the Keeper *of* Miracles

the

Keeper
of
Miracles

PHILLIP MAISEL

MACMILLAN
Pan Macmillan Australia

Pan Macmillan acknowledges the Traditional Custodians of country throughout Australia and their connections to lands, waters and communities. We pay our respect to Elders past and present and extend that respect to all Aboriginal and Torres Strait Islander peoples today. We honour more than sixty thousand years of storytelling, art and culture.

First published 2021 in Macmillan by Pan Macmillan Australia Pty Ltd
1 Market Street, Sydney, New South Wales, Australia, 2000

 A catalogue record for this book is available from the National Library of Australia

Typeset in 11/17.5pt Chronicle Text by Post Pre-press Group, Brisbane
Printed by IVE

Holocaust survivor images featured on the jacket and endpapers by Simon Shiff, provided courtesy the Jewish Holocaust Centre Melbourne
Picture section images on pages 2 (all) and 3 (C), courtesy of the Jewish Holocaust Centre Melbourne
Picture section images on pages 6 (A) and 7 (A, B, C) courtesy the Jewish Holocaust Centre archives, Phillip Maisel collection
Picture section image on page 5 (D) by Elizabeth Gilliam, State Library of Victoria
Picture section image on page 8 taken by Mark Roper
All other images courtesy the Maisel family

The author and the publisher have made every effort to contact copyright holders for material used in this book. Any person or organisation that may have been overlooked should contact the publisher.

Aboriginal and Torres Strait Islander people should be aware that this book may contain images or names of people now deceased.

For the next generation, and those
who fight for truth and justice.

Contents

I believe firmly and profoundly that whoever listens to a witness becomes a witness, so those who hear us, those who read us must continue to bear witness for us. Until now, they're doing it with us. At a certain point in time, they will do it for all of us.

– *Witness* by Elie Wiesel

Prologue

MY NAME IS PHILLIP MAISEL. FOR THE PAST thirty years, on most days of the week, I have travelled from my home to a humble museum nestled in the suburbs of Melbourne. There, in a studio, I set up my video camera and bear witness while Holocaust survivors speak about the worst days of their lives, the darkest days of the 20th century.

I record these stories for posterity. For the benefit of history. To remember the victims of the Shoah, and to speak for those who cannot speak for themselves. I do this so that others have the chance to listen to another person's story, see the world the way they do, walk for a while in their shoes.

I do this because I understand how important it is to record, for all time, what was done to innocent people in the name of a cruel ideology. To remind the world to be vigilant against bigotry and fear. So that we never forget, and it may never happen again. I do this to educate, to give people the tools they need to walk away from hatred.

I do this because I am a survivor who saw my city, my culture and my people brought to the brink of annihilation. My own story is just one of millions, but I hope that it reveals something of our shared experience. This is what stories are for—to record, for history and for all that we lost, our humanity. To understand other humans more completely. This is why we tell stories.

This is why, dear reader, I will tell you mine.

1
Building a Better World

I

I WAS BORN IN 1922 IN VILNA, A CITY WITH A COMPLI-
cated history. Today, Vilna is the capital of Lithuania,
but it has also been considered part of Poland at various
times in history.

Polish Catholicism was the majority religion in Vilna,
and it was commonly believed that Polish culture was
superior to Lithuanian. And yet, while the Lithuanian
aristocracy spoke Polish, the Polish aristocracy spoke
French, which they considered the most sophisticated
culture.

My city was a part of Poland my whole childhood, until
the Nazis came. I had been born in a time of relative
stability, following a period when, after many years of
conflict and warfare, Vilna had been annexed and incor-
porated into the second Polish republic. It was a city with
a rich political and cultural history.

Children adapt to new environments and pick up languages very easily, and at this time in history, political developments required me to learn new languages continuously.

At home, I spoke Russian (my mother's language), while at school and with my friends I spoke Polish (the official language). Polish was the most widely spoken language, followed by Yiddish, which I spoke with my relatives and people from the Jewish community. This all seemed normal to me.

Vilna was one of the greatest Jewish cities in the world at the time, and was informally known as the 'Jerusalem of the North'. Of the population of 200,000, at least 60,000 people were Jewish. Vilna's Jewish community was culturally vibrant, and home to many celebrated artists and writers. It was also somewhat unique in Europe, not only for its size, but for its liberalism. Lithuanian Judaism was profoundly influenced by a progressive 18th century rabbi, Elijah ben Solomon Zalman, who had encouraged Jews to move away from strict adherence to ritual customs and to embrace science, mathematics and western culture.

Despite the town's relatively small size, we had three newspapers to argue the discourse on issues important to the community? Prominent Jews from across Europe would come to Vilna to give lectures, and try to influence the population to take up their political cause. On any given day there would be someone trying to convert you to socialism, or convince you to join a right-wing party or take up the Zionist cause for an independent homeland for our people.

We lived in a fairly affluent part of town, but the hub of the community was in a more modest, and ancient, part of the city. The Vilna Jewish Quarter featured beautiful medieval architecture, and its artistic community made it one of the cultural centres of Europe, and a hub of theatre, literature and poetry.

All things considered, I had a very pleasant childhood. We were a comfortable middle-class family, my father made a good living exporting flax for the textile industry, and I went to a very good school. I had a brother, Joseph, six years older than me, and a twin sister, Bella, twenty minutes younger than me. From the start, she was the family favourite.

My parents had always wanted a girl, and now they had one, plus two brothers to keep her company. They were overjoyed to have a daughter, and doted on her. Bella grew up a very confident and well-liked girl, with no shortage of friends or self-esteem.

Growing up, I was close with both my siblings, and we all aimed to please our hardworking and loving parents. I will always be grateful for these happy years of our childhood, especially considering what was to come.

II

My mother and father were very much in love. My father was born in 1895 in Minsk, and when he was twenty, travelled to Poland, which was then occupied by Russia. He passed through a small town there, Horodziej, where he met my mother and they fell in love.

My paternal grandfather refused to bless the marriage, as my mother was of modest means and didn't have a dowry. This would not discourage my father, however; he left my grandfather's successful business in Minsk, worked on his own for two years until he had enough money to provide a substitute for a dowry, and then returned to marry my mother.

She was a wonderful mother, if a little strict. In our neighbourhood there were street boys my age who lived in poverty. They wore rags, and ran shoeless through the streets. They would call out, asking me to come and play, and I very much wanted to, but my mother expressly forbade it. I would have to be content with watching them play through the large window on the third floor.

Tragically, we lost my mother when I was only ten years old. She'd fallen ill with a parasitic infection, and was prescribed a dose of medicine that would be toxic to the pathogen. Sadly, the doctor gave her far too large a dose, and she did not survive.

It was devastating. We did not even know she was ill, so news of her death came as a great shock. My sister and I were away at the time, on summer holiday. We were playing out in the sunshine when suddenly my sister had a kind of fit, and insisted she needed to go home right away. She was inconsolable. Reluctantly, we took a horse-drawn cab all the way back home to discover our mother had passed away.

The lasting memory that comes to me when I think of my mother is the final visit she paid us at the holiday house. She'd come from the city to see us, then quickly returned to have her treatment. I was in bed, and she leaned over and gave me a kiss. That is the strongest lingering memory, but at least it is a comforting one.

In 1937, when I was fifteen, we visited my grandmother from my mother's side in Horodziej, where I found a collection of Russian books. Books were very precious in Poland at the time, especially books written in Russian, so this was like finding a treasure trove. Here was a wealth of schoolbooks that my mother had grown up with. Some of the books were illustrated, so I was able to match up the pictures with the Cyrillic writing, and build myself a Russian alphabet. From there, I taught myself to read in Russian, and began to read more serious works by authors such as Pushkin.

I suppose in a small way it helped me to feel closer to

my mother, being able to read these same books she had read as a girl. One looks for ways to connect to that which has been taken from us, and the moments we can do this are precious.

My father remarried eventually, to a woman named Eva Lewin, although the relationship was not driven by romance. He believed that we children needed a mother, and Eva wanted to have a family very much, so the arrangement was made. I got along with her quite well, although Bella, always the more opinionated of the two of us, took longer to warm to her.

Our home in Vilna had a very large windowsill on the third floor that looked out onto the street. I was sitting in the window one day, watching the world go by, when a little bird flew onto the windowsill and rested there for a few moments. It was a perfect scene—the little bird calmly sitting on the ledge, enjoying a sunbeam, the empty street behind it. I had a very strong desire to capture that moment, because I knew otherwise I would never be able to adequately share how it felt.

Cameras were very expensive and rare, and I could never afford to purchase one. My friend, however, had one, and she came by one day to take a photo of my sister. I distinctly recall the picture, the way Bella was posed, and the way she was framed against the sky in the photo. It was a moment of revelation for me.

To me, a camera was a way to show other people how I see the world. Everyone has a different pair of eyes, so this was a way for me to portray my individual perspective. That sense of wonder at the power of photography would never really leave me. In a photograph, you produce a slice of reality, the view from your own eyes.

III

Life became more complicated as I grew older. Poland was a majority Catholic country, with a vast, pious peasant population, and anti-Semitism was a fact of life at the time. This was unfortunately true across much of Europe. It had been that way for centuries, but in Poland it was made worse by widespread illiteracy. By the 1930s, most of the population couldn't read or write well enough to understand a newspaper. This meant peasants would get all their news at church, from priests who shared the Catholic dogma of the day. Importantly, this dogma blamed Jews for the murder of Jesus Christ. Many years later, the Pope would issue an official apology for this accusation, but that didn't help us much during those years.

Despite my comfortable life, opportunities for education by my late teens were limited because of my religion. There were only a finite number of places available for Jews at university. Whatever course you wanted to pursue—be it maths, science or medicine—a limit of 10 per cent of places in the school were allotted to Jews. The exception was agriculture, which nobody wanted to study. Poland was an agricultural country, but nobody dreamt of growing up to be an educated peasant! So, this unpopular, unglamorous industry was one of very few in which Jews were freely able to participate.

My brother Joseph, who was extremely intelligent, had no path to advance to his full potential in Poland. When he came of age he moved to France, where he would pursue electrical engineering and reach the highest standard of education available in Europe. Initially in Grenoble, then Paris, he studied at the École Supérieure, which was the highest teaching institution. De Gaulle and many other prominent members of French society attended the same university.

I attended business school, where I would have to sit on the left-hand side of the class with the other Jewish children so the teacher could identify us—and grade our work more harshly than the gentile children. I thought this was unfair; I wanted to receive the mark I believed I really deserved. Therefore, I studied so hard that I ended up becoming the best student in the class. Not because I was more talented or capable than the other boys, but because I was more stubborn. I must say though, that some of the teachers were very kind to us Jewish students, despite the prejudice of the day. My economics teacher in particular was very supportive, and nurtured my interest in studying business.

My father's plan for me was to follow in his footsteps and become a businessman. I would matriculate from school, and then travel to a university in Warsaw where a Jewish boy could secure a proper education. This was the only way for a Jew in my position to advance in Polish society at the time. That all changed when the war broke out.

IV

The people of Poland were very patriotic. There was a strong cultural appreciation for heroism, and an understanding that one of the greatest achievements possible was to sacrifice one's life for one's country. When I heard that the Soviets were sending troops into Poland, the first thing I did was volunteer to fight. I was seventeen. I ran straight to the armoury, where they gave me a rifle, surplus from World War I. The rifle was nearly as big as I was, and there was no ammunition available anywhere. I wouldn't be putting up much of a fight.

Neither would Poland. My country was not prepared to go to war. The economy was largely agricultural, with no industrial might to speak of. In fact, Poland had looked the other way when Hitler had annexed Czechoslovakia, because he'd agreed to let Poland keep a key Czechoslovakian industrial district. About two weeks before the outbreak of the war, I remember reading about the Ribbentrop–Molotov pact, the non-aggression treaty between the Third Reich and the Soviet Union.

Poland did not have the military force to defend itself, and when Hitler invaded, marking the start of World War II, the country was divided into two areas, one controlled by Germany, the other by the Soviet Union. Vilna would fall into the Soviet sphere.

On 19 September 1939, Soviet troops marched into my hometown, bringing their ideology, a new language, and a new philosophy—communism. I was young, idealistic, and believed in a new social order.

When the Soviets occupied Vilna they signed a treaty with Lithuania, putting the city under Lithuanian control. All of a sudden, we had Lithuanian Army parades going through the city centre, and attempts to make Lithuanian culture the dominant influence in Vilna. Schools that had taught in Polish suddenly had a new, Lithuanian syllabus.

I'd learned the history of Europe from a Polish perspective. Now, all the history books were rewritten, and all the Polish heroes I'd been taught to admire were recast as traitors.

The period of Lithuanian independence in Vilna lasted until 3 August 1940, when the Soviets officially annexed Vilna as part of the sixteenth Soviet republic. Now there were two official languages, Lithuanian and Russian, and all the history books were rewritten again, this time from a Soviet perspective.

During this turbulent period I sat my matriculation—the exams that would determine the sort of higher education I could pursue. At that time, schools were required to teach in Lithuanian. This was fine by me, but my examiners were not able to learn the language in such a short space of time, and spoke it less fluently than I did. As a result, I was able to give very eloquent and sensible answers to each question, and my poor teachers had to give me very high marks because they could not comprehend what I'd said.

I finished school with strong marks but wouldn't be allowed to go to university. Because I was from a wealthy family, I had been marked as ineligible for study by Soviet authorities. The communist world view separated society into three classes: workers, intelligentsia and bourgeoisie. I fell into the third class. According to Stalin's interpretation of communism, bourgeoisie families must be punished for the inequity and pain caused by the capitalist class system throughout history.

To be honest, I didn't mind—this seemed fair to me at the time. Human beings have a tendency to get swept up in ideas larger than themselves, especially young men, and I was no different.

Although my own childhood was comfortable, I was aware of a great deal of social injustice. The working class in the region generally lived in poverty. Winters sometimes fell below -20 degrees Celsius, and on Sundays I would see women from the country walking to church without shoes. Even if they could afford a pair, they could not afford to risk ruining them in the snow, so instead they would carry them over their shoulder and put them on at the church door, out of respect for the sacred ground.

One summer holidays, I befriended a local boy. Every two weeks he would appear at the local dance, have a fine time, and then disappear for a week. One day I asked him where he went every other week. He explained that he and his brother only owned one elegant pair of pants between them, and so he would wear them one week, then it would be his brother's turn. This sort of poverty was all around me growing up, and sitting down at the family dinner table, knowing that not far away a child my age was begging for bread on the street, had a profound impact on me. The inequity of society seemed fundamentally unfair, so the Soviets' enforced redistribution of wealth seemed like a remedy. The Soviet world view seemed to match my own, and Soviet propaganda was very strong, and incredibly persuasive.

For the year that the Soviets ruled Vilna, I was a devoted communist. Growing up, I genuinely believed the Soviet Union was part of a movement that was building a better world. I saw the communist doctrine of equality as a solution, not only for the poverty of the working classes, but for anti-Semitism and all forms of prejudice.

Although some Jews in Poland tended to be highly educated and civic-minded, we were still treated as second-class citizens. For centuries, anti-Semitism had been an unfortunate but unavoidable part of life in Poland. Now, all of a sudden, it was illegal.

If somebody committed an anti-Semitic act, I could report them to the police and they would be punished. Communism promised an end to inequity, not just for Jews, but for the many, many people around me enduring great hardship. If I had to make some personal sacrifices, that was fine. Who was I to take up a position at a good university when I had been born with so much? Surely there was some shoeless boy working on a farm who deserved an education more than I did.

My father was less convinced. He had been a successful merchant until the Soviets arrived, then his business was taken away from him and he was given a job at a petrol station. He saw an enormous amount of corruption and injustice under the Soviets, which I refused to open my eyes to.

We would disagree over the merits of communism, and I refused to listen to reason.

'Have you read Marx?' I would demand. 'Have you read Engels? Then how do you know what you are talking about?'

My father was a deeply tolerant man. He would listen to me ranting about my love for Marx with good humour, then would politely disagree with me and try to get on with life.

The Soviets implemented a policy designed to provide housing for everyone. For every four square metres of floor space in a home, one person would be assigned to live there.

This meant two more families would move into our large, comfortable house. One day it was just me, my sister, father and stepmother, and the next the place was crowded with strangers. Before long my father became good friends with one of the women who had moved in, Maria Grodnizka, who would have been in her early forties, and life continued to be fairly stable.

V

Instead of going to university, I began working as the manager of a stationery store. There was a similar store not far away, and I became good friends with a fellow who worked there, Hirsch Glick. We were a similar age, and we were both members of a communist trade union. The two of us were young, and wanted to build a new world, and we were sure communism was the way to do it.

Because I could read and write Russian, I was promoted to the position of technical secretary of the trade union, and would keep notes for our Soviet supervisors. They kept a very close eye on everything we did. The trade union had certain expectations of the workers. Before each public holiday, when we were supposed to have a day off, there would always be the same little performance at our meeting. One worker would forward a motion that we work through the day, as a show of patriotic duty to the communist cause. Then he would ask who was for or against it. We would all sigh, but of course we had to vote in favour of working for free.

Each Thursday evening at 8 pm we attended compulsory weekly communist indoctrination meetings. Afterwards, Hirsch and I would walk along the banks of the river and talk about writing and poetry. Hirsch was a poet, already well known for his work, and I hung on his every word. I'd been interested in poetry at school, and in any case, Hirsch was a very interesting person. He was an introvert, a dreamy young man, and a very quiet and calm presence. I had never met anyone quite like him, and never would again.

On our walks I would ask him for advice on writing poetry. The way he wrote was extraordinary—he would compose his poems entirely in his head, just holding the whole thing in his mind, sometimes for months. Then, one day, when he was sure it was perfect, he would write it down, without changing a word, and would never touch it again. Once it was written, that was the final version. He was an inspiration to me, and to many other idealistic young people in Vilna at the time.

I had a couple of schoolfriends who had been even more enthusiastic about communism than I was, and had run away to the Soviet Union a couple of years earlier. After the creation of the Lithuanian Soviet Republic, they returned, wearing the same coats and boots they had left in two years earlier.

'Why haven't you bought new clothes in all this time?' I wanted to know. They explained that it was impossible, that there were desperate shortages of everything in Russia: clothes, food, medicine. My friends and I thought they were being provocateurs; that they had been engaged by the Soviet secret police to get us to say something incriminating about Russia, so we could be arrested and sent to forced labour camps in Siberia. With the strength of Soviet propaganda, it seemed impossible that the situation in Russia could be so bad. Of course, we were wrong: living conditions across the border were terrible.

We weren't wrong to be paranoid about the secret police, however. They were a constant fact of life under Soviet rule, something you had to think about at all times. When my father and I would walk on the street we would talk very quietly to each other, just in case we said something that could be interpreted as anti-Soviet.

No deviation from the official Soviet opinion was tolerated. If a Soviet agent were to ask me what I thought of Trotsky (who Stalin considered an enemy of the state), for example, I would have to answer in exactly the same phrasing as the official Soviet propaganda. It took considerable effort to remember the accepted opinion, word for word, on every issue.

Even a true believer like me could easily attract trouble. One time, I was nearly arrested and sent to a Siberian Gulag for being too good at my job at the stationery store. I'd realised I could save money and turn a greater profit if I stocked up on paper while it was cheap, so I amassed an enormous amount of paper in the storeroom. A few months later, Vilna was experiencing a shortage of paper, and the price increased considerably. Because I had a lot of paper, my shop became the most profitable in the city.

I was very proud of my work making money for the Soviet state, but one Thursday, the secret police arrived. I normally stayed a half hour after the store closed to tidy up, and that's when they knocked on the door.

'Why is your store making so much profit?' one of them wanted to know.

I explained that I had a surplus, and so business was good. They didn't like that at all.

'But comrade,' the policeman said, 'don't you realise that by holding onto extra stock you're depriving all the other shops of their profit?'

I didn't know what to say. There was no correct answer. No matter how I tried to explain myself, they only became more hostile. I thought I would be put in chains on the spot, but luckily the phone rang. It was a member of my trade union, checking to see if the meeting was at 8 pm, as usual. The police listened in, then realised I was secretary of the union. Arresting me would only get them into trouble, so they left.

In time, I did begin to identify a few flaws with the Soviet occupation, and decided to write a letter to Stalin detailing some of my criticisms. I was that naïve. Luckily, I lost the letter before I put it in the mail. If I'd sent that letter I would have been off to Siberia before the glue on the stamp could dry!

Shortages of basic goods and supplies grew more

frequent during the time of Soviet rule, and social services and the quality of medical care were harder to maintain. My poor stepmother, Eva, passed away in 1940 while hospitalised with meningitis. It was a very sad development for our family, but we resolved to persevere. We could not know what the future would hold for us.

VI

Three weeks before Germany invaded the Soviet Union, the Soviets rounded up everybody who was judged to be an enemy of the state and put them on a train to Siberia. This included intelligentsia and bourgeoisie, but also regular people who believed more strongly in pure socialism than Soviet-style communism.

That kind of paranoia and internal repression was commonplace across Soviet territories. Stalin's cult of personality was so strong that it could tolerate no criticism or alternate ideology.

My father assured me that if war did break out, the Soviets would protect their interests in Lithuania and we would be safe. Even though we had received word of anti-Semitic attacks in Germany, my father did not believe that Hitler's hatred extended to all Jews, just the German ones. Human beings are mysterious entities—even the smartest of us will cling to delusions when the reality is too difficult to face. My father was one of the wisest men I ever knew, but somehow he, and many like him, could not bring himself to believe the truth about Nazi Germany.

But then, in a pre-Holocaust world, how could he possibly imagine what was to come? It seemed unreasonable that the same Germany that had produced Goethe, Schiller, Beethoven, Bach and Brahms could be capable of what it proved itself to be.

Lithuanian Jewry had assumed that Hitler would not touch them. They were wrong.

On 22 June 1941, the Nazis launched a surprise attack on Soviet forces: Operation Barbarossa. The Soviets were taken so completely by surprise that Stalin refused to believe Hitler had turned on him, and did not order counterattacks for some time. The Soviet air force and army in Lithuania were caught on the ground and destroyed by Luftwaffe bombers. The Soviets could not defend us.

In Vilna, we were horrified. My sister, myself, our housemate Maria Grodnizka and her brother decided to try to escape for the Soviet border. Father, who was suspicious of the Soviets, decided he trusted the Germans more than the Russians, and stayed behind. He'd lived through the German occupation of Vilna in 1917, when the Germans had treated the local Jews much better than the Russian armies that followed. So, we said goodbye, unsure when we would see each other again.

For three days we travelled on foot towards the border, but the German tanks were faster, and overtook us. We knew that if we kept travelling in the open we would be killed, so we decided to turn back. Along the way we took shelter at the home of a white Russian washer-woman who used to visit us every month and take our laundry for cleaning. My mother had once intervened on behalf of the woman's son, who'd been arrested for petty theft. He was going to prison until my mother vouched for him and paid for legal representation. When we knocked on her door, she hurried us inside and invited us to stay the night. She gave us some soup, and we were so famished and so grateful for her very simple soup that she started to cry.

We returned to the city, which was in the process of being occupied by German troops. They were not interested in us—they each had orders to occupy a section of the city, and small battalions marched off in separate directions. It was like watching a machine operate.

I ran straight home, fearing for my father's life, and found him sitting on the staircase of our apartment, distraught. It had been only seven days since I'd last seen him, but he was grey, and looked ten years older. We promised one another we would never part again.

VII

The first thing the Nazis used to strip us of our humanity was the yellow star. We were forced to register on a list of Lithuanian Jews, and to wear the yellow star marking us as Jewish wherever we went. With the star came many restrictions on basic civil liberties.

Then they created the Ghetto. The Nazi leadership selected a site in the medieval part of Vilna's old town for the Ghetto. It was a modest, traditionally Jewish neighbourhood, and from the formation of the Ghetto it would be a prison for us. The Nazis, at this stage of their conquest of Europe, feared resistance and armed rebellion from Jewish populations in occupied cities. They also needed vast quantities of forced labour, which they sought from Jewish people in subjugated cities. Ghettos were established in many cities—walled prisons in which Jewish populations could be observed, controlled and exploited for labour.

To justify the formation of the Vilna Ghetto, the Nazis staged a provocative incident on 31 August 1941, in which Lithuanians in civilian clothes pretended to shoot at German soldiers, then fled into an apartment building owned by Jews. German soldiers used the incident as an excuse to seize two random Jews, beat them, and shoot them on the spot.

An anti-Jewish riot began, and that night, Jews were driven out of the site of the future Ghetto, arrested, and taken to prison, then to Ponary Forest, where between 5000 and 10,000 of them were murdered.

The Nazis split the old town into two discrete Ghettos, one large and one small. From 6–7 September the Nazis tracked down 20,000 Jews from across the city, evicting them from their homes and herding them into the Ghettos. Those who had converted or married a Jewish spouse were taken too. Prominent Jews were arrested by Nazis who demanded enormous ransoms in order to secure their freedom from the Ghetto. Leaders of the Jewish community went from house to house as they collected all the gold, jewellery and other valuables they could gather. The Nazis took the ransom payment, then claimed it was insufficient and shot them anyway. Many important leaders of the Jewish community, were executed in this way.

On 7 September, at 4 pm, a Lithuanian auxiliary soldier knocked on our door.

'Pack your things!' he barked. 'You have twenty minutes to be downstairs. Take only what you can carry.'

There was no time to pack a bag, or even think about what we might need. My father very cleverly put bedsheets down on the floor, piled as much food and clothing as we could carry onto them, and tied them up as a bundle. These bundles were just large enough for us to carry, as we started to walk towards the Large Ghetto. Maria, my father, my sister and I joined a slow-moving procession—all Jews, carrying whatever they could—walking towards the Ghetto. (Maria's brother left us, running for the Russian border, thinking he would survive more easily on his own. He was never seen again and we never learned of his fate.) But by the time we arrived, the Lithuanian and German soldiers had already closed the gate. They told us that the Ghetto was full, and they wouldn't be letting anyone else in. They advised us that on the other side of the Ghetto there was another gate that was still accepting people, so we rushed to get there, only to be told the same thing. Nobody else would be allowed into the Ghetto.

This was as good as a death sentence. Anyone wearing a yellow star caught on the street after curfew would be arrested and executed. Already, it was almost night. We were in a crowd of almost 2000 Jews who had been locked out, and it wouldn't be long until the Lithuanian troops started arresting us. My father was in despair—this was the most frightened and unsafe we'd felt since the start of the war. We sat down in a narrow laneway between two buildings to try and work out what to do.

Then—a miracle. Maria noticed that at the end of the laneway, someone had left a ground-floor window open. One by one, ten of us scrambled through the window. We found ourselves in a narrow hallway with a staircase at one end, and hurried up it.

At the top was a small, empty room, pitch black, with no windows and no exits. We were trying to decide what to do when we heard footsteps in the hall below. Someone had seen us climb through the window, and now soldiers were searching the house. Heavy boots thudded on the floor-boards as one of the soldiers started mounting the stairs. We had nowhere to go and nothing to hide behind, ten of us crammed into the tiny room.

We flattened ourselves against the walls as the door swung open and a young Lithuanian soldier came in. He could not see us in the dark, his hand grasping the wall like a man looking for a light switch in a strange room. The soldier started searching along the wall with one hand, the other resting on the trigger on his rifle. We didn't dare breathe, and the only sound was his footsteps getting closer to where we stood flat against the wall. Then, his hand touched my arm.

There was a long moment while he paused, and then he kept walking, touching each of us one by one, making sure that we were in the room. I squeezed my eyes shut, expecting a bullet. Instead, he walked back to the door and called down the stairs.

'Nobody here,' he yelled down. 'Let's keep looking.'

None of us could believe it. When we were sure it was safe, we left the dark room and stared at each other in wonder. We should all be in prison, or worse, but by some miracle we had been found by a Lithuanian soldier whose sense of right and wrong, his basic humanity, had made him decide not to turn us in.

We found a path to the attic and were able to make it to the roof. If I looked down onto the street, I could see the Lithuanian soldiers starting to lead away all the poor souls who had been trapped outside the Ghetto. None of them would live much longer.

The houses in the old Jewish quarter were very tightly packed together, so we were able to jump from rooftop to rooftop until we found another open window in a building just inside the Ghetto. We were met with chaos, as a dozen families who'd been uprooted from their homes and forced into the cramped Ghetto wept and tried to come to terms with what was happening. This would be my home for the next two years.

2
In the Ghetto

I

THE GATE OF THE VILNA GHETTO HAD A SIGN outside it: *'Achtung! Seuchengefahr!'*—'Attention! Danger of infection!'

The sign, like the Ghetto, served two purposes—to segregate us from the rest of society, and to dehumanise us in the eyes of the Polish community. The sign warned the people of Vilna, who were already suspicious of Jews, that we were unclean and unsafe to live alongside.

The truth is, conditions inside the Ghetto *were* unsafe. The Vilna Ghetto, like other Jewish Ghettos created by Nazi Germany, were deliberately designed to ensure overcrowded, impoverished and inhumane conditions.

It would have been physically impossible to crowd any more people into the Ghetto. The number of people living in an apartment was exactly as many people as could lie on the floor like sardines in a tin. To cross the apartment to get from the kitchen to the toilet, one had to carefully step across all the people lying on the floor.

Each family crammed into our apartment was allowed to use the stove for only a few minutes a day, and there was no fuel to cook with, aside from wastepaper. You would try to get a fire going using old paper, quickly heat your meal, and move on for the next person to cook before the fire died out.

We were lucky in one way. My father had packed up all the grains we had in the house, including a large container of barley. That saved us from going hungry on many evenings—this humble little grain that, when cooked, would expand to many times its size. My father estimated we had enough to last maybe two months, but every time we went to cook more, it would swell up, and it never seemed to run out. The supply we brought into the Ghetto was enough to feed us through the leanest times, of which there would be many. From our first day in the Ghetto until the ordeal of the European Jews finally ended, there was not a day when I had enough to eat.

Despite the best efforts of the Nazis, conditions were never as bad as they might have been. The Jewish community of Vilna had a particularly distinguished medical tradition, and those doctors who survived the first round of mass murder worked hard to maintain public health within the Ghetto walls. Others worked to keep morale up—the cultural life of the ghetto stayed strong, with public lectures, poetry, and theatrical productions.

My friend Hirsch Glick was very involved in the artistic community as a poet. Literature thrived inside the Ghetto. One of the most important buildings within its walls was the Straszuna Library—one of the greatest Jewish libraries in Europe, and now the centre of the Ghetto's cultural life. Jews trapped in the Ghetto turned to reading for solace, and when the library lent out its 100,000th book, a celebration was organised. A newspaper was also regularly published—journalists would write it by hand and hang it up on the wall so that people could visit and read the news of the day.

The Ghetto was run by the *Judenrät*, or 'Jewish council', a kind of puppet government of Jewish leaders installed by the Germans. Jews were required to form a *Judenrät* in every Ghetto. As a rule, the *Judenräts* of Europe provided the Germans with a means to manipulate inhabitants of the Ghetto, and Vilna was no exception. It also gave them collaborators as they began to slowly dismantle our community.

A Lithuanian Jew and former military officer named Jacob Gens was the head of the Vilna Ghetto's Jewish government. He attempted to secure better conditions and safety for some citizens in the Ghetto, and mistakenly believed that collaborating with the Germans could save some lives. Gens and his policemen rounded up Jews in the first *aktionen*, 'actions', in which Ghetto residents were arrested and deported for execution, and he would try to barter with Nazi leadership. They would ask him to organise 5000 Jews to be sent to labour camps, and he would try to convince them to accept, say, 3000 instead. It was futile, and he was a divisive figure within the Ghetto.

While few trusted Gens, there were very fine people working under him who tried to do their best for the Jews. Maria Grodnizka was one of them. She had a position working for a key member of the *Judenrät*, who was able to quietly arrange for many lives to be saved.

Ever since the Ghetto was first established, German and Lithuanian task forces would conduct surprise purges.

One system introduced that supported such purges was the 'Yellow Pass Action', in which the Germans assigned distinctive yellow certificates to 3000 workers and three members of their families. These allowed Jews who were certified as valuable workers to leave the Ghetto to work. Anyone without these passes was in danger of being snatched up.

These Actions usually happened on Jewish holidays.

The Nazis had specialists in Jewish customs within their ranks, who instructed troops to persecute us on the days when we would least expect it. On 1 October 1941—Yom Kippur, the Day of Atonement, which is perhaps the most solemn and sacred holy day for Jews—the Germans arrested nearly 2000 people who were found without work permits. They were all murdered.

Later that month, the Nazis liquidated the Small Ghetto, where 'unproductive' individuals, such as the elderly, the ill, and the intellectuals who they considered unfit for labour, were housed. The message was clear: if you were not of use to the Reich, you would not be allowed to live.

To get the correct papers to survive, it was important to find work that the Germans considered indispensable. If they valued your labour you had a greater chance of survival, even though they did not value your humanity.

My father had an old friend who worked in *Heereskraftfahrpark* 562—also called HKP—an engineering unit that bore the brunt of the mechanical work involved in keeping German cars and trucks working. One day, he mentioned to my father that the facility was looking for auto-electricians.

'Do you know of any auto-electricians we could hire?'

'Certainly,' my father said. 'My son is a very accomplished auto-electrician.'

This was an exaggeration. To say I was an auto-electrician was a stretch. I knew how to repair a fuse if the radio in our old home needed it, but that was about it.

Technically speaking, I had never looked under the bonnet of a car. Before the Nazi occupation, cars were comparatively rare in Vilna. There were public buses, but cars were scarce enough that when I was a child, if I'd seen one on the way to school, I would mention it at the dinner table: 'Would you believe it? I saw a car today!'

Nevertheless, they hired me, awarded me a special pass, and set me to work at a branch of HKP—a highly sought-after work detail in the Ghetto.

The foreman there didn't seem bothered that I knew nothing about cars. He put me to work sweeping the workshop. This was a futile task, as the workshop had an earthen floor. I could sweep the dirt all day and it would still be dirt.

The foreman was a good man that way. He was also a very fine mechanic. German army cars would arrive from the battlefront in various states of ruin. It was our task to fix them, but often specific car parts would be damaged beyond repair, and the Germans were happy to scrap them.

Whenever a car part was beyond repair, the foreman would dismantle it and salvage the components for his own inventions. Using scrap copper and salvaged gears from ruined cars, he invented an electrical generator, which he attached to the doors of one of the most frequently visited buildings in the Aryan sector of Vilna—the church. Each day, the church doors would open and close hundreds of times, and the motion from that would be converted into electricity and stored in a battery hidden beneath the church. He then sold that invention to the church, so they could keep the lights on when electricity was scarce.

I began dismantling car parts that had been marked as scrap to try and work out how they were built, and how they could be repaired. A little at a time, through experience, I began to develop new skills.

Our apartment happened to be on the same street as the Straszuna Library. After work I could go down to the library, which was full of textbooks and technical manuals. I found detailed diagrams of starter motors, the electrical wiring of modern cars—everything I needed to educate myself.

It didn't take long for me to become a very skilled auto-electrician. It actually worked to my advantage that I didn't have a formal education, as it meant I hadn't been taught what was considered possible and what wasn't. Because nobody instructed me otherwise, I found ways to repair things that theoretically couldn't be repaired. Take the fuel gauge for the radiator—other electricians wouldn't waste their time, and would simply throw them away when they blew, but I had access to three or four of the same damaged parts and could dismantle and rebuild a gauge that was as good as one that had just come off the factory floor.

II

As an extra level of insurance for our safety, my father organised false Aryan identity papers for our family, as well as for Maria. They were produced by experts in forgery within the Ghetto, and they were very expensive. These allowed Bella and Maria to move out of the Ghetto, assuming the identity of a Polish national.

It was very taxing to live that way. It was terribly hard to live under the cover of a false identity. Wherever Bella and Maria went, they encountered anti-Semitic propaganda posters, and overheard cruel jokes about Jews in the street. Now and again they would come back to stay with us in the Ghetto and recover, sometimes for months at a time. The conditions in the Ghetto were very confronting when you weren't used to them, and Bella often cried at night. But where else could they go for respite from the reign of terror that made life in the Aryan sector impossible for Jews?

All it would take was for one person to recognise them and denounce them to the authorities and that would be the end. It's extremely difficult to stay alert to the danger all around you. The stress of living that way accumulates with each passing day. You grow weary, and you start to make mistakes.

One day, a beautiful spring morning, it grew so warm in the workshop that I took off my jacket, which had the yellow star attached. I went outside to run an errand, and saw an old Polish schoolfriend of mine walking in my direction. My first instinct was to wave, then I realised I wasn't wearing my yellow star. He knew I was Jewish. If I drew too much attention to myself, he might denounce me to the Nazis and that would be that. I tried to stay calm and kept walking, and my friend and I passed each other without nodding. To this day I don't know if he failed to recognise me, or if he did, but ignored me to keep me safe. Either way, it was a close call.

It was illegal for me to fraternise with someone who wasn't Jewish outside of a professional situation. As far as the authorities were concerned, I could leave the Ghetto only to work at the workshop I was assigned to. That didn't stop people, though.

The workshop was surrounded by residential buildings, with Polish civilians living inside them. Occasionally, people would approach me and ask me to do some electrical work for them; repairing appliances or installing electric lights in their homes. In return, they would usually pay me in food or other goods. This was a risk for both parties. If the Nazis caught Polish civilians using up the time of one of their Jewish labourers, they would be punished. Of course, my punishment would be much worse. If I were to be caught, I would be beaten, possibly killed, but the rewards made the risk seem worth it.

Occasionally I had trouble connecting an apartment to the electricity grid, so I had to go to the neighbour and ask if I could connect to their power supply. This in itself was dangerous, because any Polish person could identify me as a Jew at a glance. If I knocked on an anti-Semite's door, they could denounce me and that would be that. Somehow, I never knocked on the wrong door—either I was very fortunate, or people were generally just happy to try and survive.

A young couple who had recently married wanted me to install an electric light in their room, above the bed. Their building was not particularly well made, and the material on the ceiling was too unstable to properly install a light. I advised them against it.

'I don't know if it's safe,' I told them.

'We told you to do it,' said the husband. 'Just do it.'

That night, sure enough, the lamp fell down. The newly-weds were furious with me, and accused me of doing a poor job. They threatened to go to the authorities. I had to think quickly.

'No, no,' I said. I explained that I'd done a good job, that they must have been jumping on the bed to make the light collapse. I asked them to tell me what they had been doing that shook the walls of the house. The newlyweds were suddenly very shy, and accepted my explanation without further complaint.

Anything you needed had to be traded for. When my shoes proved inadequate for the task of working on my feet all day, my father managed to trade a few of his precious belongings for a pair of sturdy French army boots from World War I. They were a little too large for me, but they would come to be the most precious asset I could imagine owning.

III

Even the ability to come and go from the Ghetto was an invaluable asset. For those inside without papers, who were unable to trade with the outside world, the help of a go-between was worth a great deal. We were banned from bringing many items, including most foods, into the Ghetto. The guards would randomly search everyone coming in and out, confiscate any contraband food, and savagely beat anyone caught trying to smuggle it in.

One important exception to this rule was milk. We were allowed milk, so every day when I went out, I would buy two bottles of milk at work. Then I would bring this back into the Ghetto, and trade it to another family. The profit I made off that one bottle was enough to buy milk for my entire family.

The Nazis were not the only danger. They were reinforced by some 13,000 Lithuanian Auxiliary Police—soldiers who had allied with the Germans, who they considered a liberating force from Soviet rule. They ruled the streets outside the Ghetto, while inside, we were kept under control by the Jewish Police.

The Jewish Police were special auxiliary police units organised by the *Judenrät*. Their job was to uphold Nazi law within the Ghetto, and to discourage resistance in any form. In return for collaborating, they were given extra food and privileges—and, most importantly, their families were kept safe from Actions.

They did not have uniforms, just an identifying hat, armband and badge. They weren't allowed to carry guns, but they were given batons, and the authority to use them on other Jews.

Many Jews saw any cooperation with the oppressor as immoral. Some were so angry they were willing to fight. The United Partisan Organisation, or *Fareynikte Partizaner Organizatsye* (FPO) in Yiddish, was the official resistance authority of the Vilna Ghetto. It was formed in early 1942 by non-official Jewish leaders who refused to go like sheep to the slaughter.

The resistance was not one unified group. It consisted of several smaller groups, each drawn from pre-occupation political parties. Five or six political factions made up different wings of the FPO. Jews from opposite sides of the ideological spectrum, who had been sworn enemies before the Nazi invasion, now united to stand against the common foe.

Each group was further divided into a cell of only a few people, and within that cell, each person would know the identity of only one or two other people. This was a safety measure against capture; if the Nazis caught you, they would torture you until gave up your compatriots. Keeping us insulated from each other meant that even if we broke under torture, we could not denounce more than a couple of members.

I shared a political cell with Hirsch Glick. He was a peaceful soul, but became increasingly radicalised due to the maltreatment of Jews. He had been sent to work at a labour camp called Rzesza, but was brought back to the Vilna Ghetto after that camp was liquidated. It was then that he wrote the poem 'Partisans' Song', *Zog Nit Keynmol*. Later it was set to the melody of a Soviet hymn, and it became a very famous resistance anthem after the war. It has been said that Hirsch wrote 'Partisans' Song' while the Warsaw Ghetto uprising was taking place, but from the Vilna Ghetto we could not have known about those events. I believe, however, that the poem was actually written for a specific partisan—a young Jewish partisan girl with whom Hirsch was in love.

I remember the day Hirsch debuted the poem. We were in a cellar located on Straszuna Street. I was present with my sister, Bella, together with Moisze, who had been the secretary of our trade union. Hirsch read the poem to us in the light of a candle. It was extraordinary.

That same night he read another poem he'd written about the female partisan Vitka Kempner, who'd blown up a German train full of soldiers and munitions. I suppose he was a little in love with her. Hirsch was not nearly as excited about 'Partisans' Song' as he was about this poem, but it was embraced by the resistance and took on a life of its own.

Whenever we saw an opportunity, we would sabotage the industrial and military facilities of the Nazis. Some of us began using German facilities to create and stock-pile weapons, so we could defend the Ghetto when the time came.

The makeshift weapons we had been creating were a sort of homemade acid grenade. We would take a glass light globe, carefully fill it with battery acid, and then seal it off with a bit of lead welding. If I were to find myself in conflict with an enemy soldier, I could throw it in his face, blind him, and seize his weapon while he was incapacitated.

My other major contribution to our arsenal was smuggling fuel rods into the Ghetto. The Russian trucks I was working on were built with a heavy steel bar reinforcing the fuel tank. Whenever possible, I would steal this from a truck I was working on and bring it into the Ghetto so we could use it as a club when armed conflict began. This gives you an idea of our idealism—we thought we could defend ourselves against machine guns with metal rods.

The resistance became badly demoralised when we lost one of our leaders in early 1943. Yitzhak Wittenberg was the head of the FPO until a member of the underground was caught, and denounced him under torture. The *Judenrät* attempted to turn Wittenberg over to the Gestapo, and during the argument gunfire broke out between Jewish Police and FPO fighters. Wittenberg managed to escape, and went into hiding.

His initial escape caused a rift in the Ghetto. The *Judenrät* and most older people wanted Wittenberg to turn himself in, potentially saving thousands of people from German reprisal. Mobs went door to door searching for him. They didn't find him, however—he still had the sympathies of the FPO and young radicals inside the Ghetto, who helped him disguise himself as a woman and stay out of sight.

Ultimately, Wittenberg decided that the safety of Ghetto prisoners was worth more than his own life, and turned himself in to the Gestapo. He was found dead in his cell the next morning. The rumour was that Gens had slipped him a cyanide pill at their last meeting.

After that, many FPO members slipped out of the city to join the partisan groups massing in the forest around Vilna. By the end of the year, the liquidation of the Ghetto would begin. Gens' efforts to save some of us had been foolish, and served only to weaken our capacity to fight back. For his service to the Germans, he was ordered to report to Gestapo headquarters, where he was shot. One of his final actions as Jewish leader was to attempt to take control of the liquidation, to keep Nazi forces out of the Ghetto and away from a partisan ambush. Instead, Estonian troops allied to the Nazis were brought in. They arrested and deported us, and served as our overseers in prison camps in Nazi-occupied Estonia.

IV

On 23 September 1944, the Nazis began the liquidation, and we knew it was time to fight. Before dawn, Estonian troops had surrounded the Ghetto, with intent to liquidate it. At best, Jews could hope to be sent to labour camps, where they would be brutalised and treated as slaves. It was time to rebel.

A knock at the door at four in the morning let me know the uprising had begun. A fellow I'd never seen before nodded at me.

'Rivka called,' he said. This was the codeword to signal that it was time to go to war. My father implored me not to go out, to take shelter with him in the bunker we had built in the basement of the Ghetto, but I would not listen. I wanted to fight.

Word quickly spread among FPO members all over the Ghetto. The resistance quickly split into two armed battalions. One would try to seize the hospital inside the Ghetto, as we would need it for the fight ahead. The other would take a stand in the town square that bordered on the Aryan sector. I was in this group, and I took my place among around 200 partisan fighters. My only weapons were three of my homemade acid grenades.

We were brave, but were outgunned. While we were still gathering, Estonian soldiers armed with machine guns suddenly appeared on two sides of the square, effectively surrounding us.

At gunpoint, they instructed us to march backwards, and we began to comply. I was moving a little more slowly than the rest of the crowd, and managed to slip away to where a line of small houses lined the square. I jumped through an open window and quickly hid in a cupboard, knowing there was a good chance one of the soldiers had seen me.

Sure enough, I heard an Estonian soldier walk up to the window. It creaked as he stuck his head in to look around the room. Seeing nobody, he moved on.

As soon as it was safe, I sneaked back onto the street and hurried to the hospital, where the resistance fighters were supposed to be taking a stand. I hammered on the door, yelling out my name and that I needed to come in and fight. After a moment, a man answered in Yiddish.

'Look!' he said. 'We've barricaded the door. We're not going to take it down just to let you in, so buzz off!'

I didn't know where else to go—enemy soldiers were all over the place, hunting down FPO fighters. Now and again you would hear gunshots rattle through the streets as skirmishes broke out. I had to get out of the open.

Outside the hospital was a giant pile of firewood used to run the furnaces. I climbed up and over the woodpile, and found a spot where I could hide from patrols while keeping an eye on the street below. While I was moving wood to make a better hiding spot, I uncovered an axe. Holding the axe, I lay very still, and waited.

Perhaps fifteen minutes passed before I saw a lone Estonian soldier walking down the road, peering in windows with his rifle slung loosely over one arm. He wasn't paying attention to the wood pile, and passed right by without noticing me there, gripping the axe.

I knew that I could kill him easily, take his weapon and join the fight, but at the last moment I decided not to. Killing that one Estonian soldier might mean the death of many, many Jews. The Nazis had a policy of retribution for armed insurrection. Any act of violence against Axis soldiers would be punished by rounding up and murdering random Jews. Women and children were fair game—in this, the Nazis did not discriminate.

So I let him pass by. As I did, a door slammed open on the street just behind him. A little girl, maybe eight years old, rushed out to ambush the soldier. Would you believe it, she also had an axe, a tiny little hatchet that she meant to kill the soldier with. He saw her, smiled, and easily disarmed her, then turned her around and gave her a gentle kick on the behind.

'Go home,' he told her. 'It's not safe out here.'

She ran back inside and slammed the door. Seconds later, more Estonian soldiers appeared, and I felt such overwhelming relief that I had not killed the fellow. If I'd done so, the next patrol would have surely killed me, and probably that little girl and her whole family, too.

Just as importantly, the way the soldier had refused to harm the little girl reminded me he was human. He was a scared young man in the middle of a war, just like me. If a minute ago I'd felt guilty for not murdering him, I now realised I'd never have forgiven myself if I had. That was as close to committing violence as I would come for the whole war. I just didn't have it in me. Perhaps that is weakness, perhaps it is strength. In any case, I am glad I didn't go down that route. I have never regretted it.

V

Once the coast was clear, I went to see what was happening elsewhere in the city. I came across a Jewish policeman, who told me I was under arrest.

'I'm working for the Germans,' I told him, producing my work permit. 'You can't arrest me.'

He took my papers, glanced at them and tore them up. 'Today, papers don't matter.'

Grabbing my arm, he marched me to the gate, where the Nazis searched my clothing and found the improvised acid grenades. Furious, they threw them on the ground, where they bounced harmlessly off the cobblestones. I felt terrible. These weapons that I'd thought were so clever didn't even work!

The Nazis put me on a little truck to take me to the police for processing. There were already a few other boys on the truck who'd also been arrested.

As the truck rumbled through the streets I thought about the time, after I first joined the FPO, when I'd been approached by a resistance fighter named Jascha Raff, who was recruiting young men to join the partisans encamped in the forest around Vilna.

I had to say no. It was too dangerous. The forest was maybe ten kilometres away from Vilna, so even if we found our way through the sewers and outside the city walls, there would be a treacherous stretch of occupied open space to get through without being seen.

Besides, I had to look after my father. Whatever happened next, I felt I had a better chance of survival than my ageing father. I had a responsibility to look after him, so I turned down the offer. Now I wondered what difference it would have made in the end, having found myself under arrest anyway.

The truck arrived at Vilna train station, where they searched us thoroughly. Then we waited, as many more prisoners arrived on other trucks. I searched their faces to see if any of my friends were among them, and suddenly

I recognised Jascha, the young man who had asked me to join the partisans in the forest. Our eyes met, and he looked away before the soldiers could see we were acquainted.

They searched him, and found that he had a gun. Before he had a chance to use it, they shot him on the spot. He was twenty-one years old.

That was deeply traumatic for me—this was the first time I had seen a friend killed, much less shot at point blank range in front of me. Unfortunately, it would not be the last.

The soldiers loaded us onto the train, eighty people to a wagon, counting us off as we climbed into the carriage. The soldier in charge announced that we would be counted again when the train reached its destination.

'If there are less than eighty people in this wagon on the other end, all of you will be shot. Remember that if you think about trying to escape,' he said. He slammed the door on the wagon that would take me away from Vilna, and my family, leaving us in darkness.

3

Small Miracles

I

I T WAS DARK IN THE WAGON, WHICH WAS PART OF A CARGO
train originally built for cattle, and crowded, and hot, even
when it was cold outside. For three days and three nights
we travelled deeper into Nazi territory. We were each given
one loaf of bread and one bottle of water to last us the three
days. In the corner was a single bucket, which all eighty of us,
men and women alike, had to use as a toilet. By the end of
the journey, it was very unpleasant indeed inside that train.

Three days' journey brought us to a transport hub at
Auvere in Estonia, where many people from all over Eastern
Europe were already encamped after arriving on previous
transports. After a few hours we were ordered to march to
Waivira, where we would join other prisoners working on
a massive, somewhat desperate initiative by the Nazis to
recover from the disastrous loss at the Battle of Stalingrad.

In February 1943, the German armies at Stalingrad

had surrendered. After six months, nearly two million casualties, and the deaths of countless civilians, the battle was over. Nearly a million German troops had been taken prisoner, and their Luftwaffe and panzer divisions were shattered. Those tanks and planes that remained required tremendous amounts of fuel. Without their vehicles, the Nazis had no hope of winning the war, so they were desperately searching for alternative fuel sources across the annexed territories.

To this end, the Germans rushed the development of experimental technology to extract oil from shale rock deposits.

Waivira was part of this shale-mining initiative, a forced labour camp in Estonia where those imprisoned by the Nazis were used as slave labour to mine shale rock from which oil could theoretically be extracted.

It was the first real labour camp I'd seen, surrounded on all sides by barbed wire. Two guards stood at the gate, an Estonian policeman in full uniform, and a Jewish policeman wearing his armband. As I walked up, I saw the Jewish policeman offer the Estonian a cigarette, and light it for him. It was one of the most demoralising things I'd seen for months. This Estonian was the enemy of my nation, the same regime that had destroyed our Ghetto and enabled the Nazis to murder my friend, and here was a Jew giving him a cigarette.

The camp was unprepared for the number of arrivals being transported, and there were no barracks to house us. Initially we had to sleep on the ground, with only the shirts on our backs and a flimsy tent overhead to protect us from the freezing cold. We tried to keep warm by lying as close to each other as possible.

By chance, I was billeted with thirty people from Vilna who were members of my resistance group—we'd all been arrested on the same day, and so ended up in the same camp. So at least I had my friends.

The prisoners had to build their own barracks. Each day we would walk a few hundred metres away from the camp, where we were tasked with constructing the housing for our own prison. A truck would arrive with pre-fabricated building materials, which we would then assemble and erect.

I hoped that the Nazi trucks would break down—if one were to fail, they would need a mechanic, and would call on me. Unfortunately this never happened, though it would be my skill with automobiles that got me out of that camp in the end.

II

One day, two *Schutzstaffel* (SS) men arrived at our tent looking for auto-mechanics. The SS were a paramilitary branch of the German armed forces, responsible for the administration of the forced labour, concentration, and extermination camps. They were instantly recognisable by their black uniforms, and infamous for their cruelty.

The SS asked the Jewish leader of our group if there were any mechanics among us. I saw an opportunity, and identified myself as an auto-electrician. Our leader looked me over.

'Can you change a tyre?' he asked.

My heart sank. I had no idea how to change a tyre. All my training involved the electrical machinery of the car; the mechanical side was somewhat of a mystery to me. I was standing there, trying to decide what to say, when he spoke again.

'What a stupid question. Of course you can change a tyre.' And with that, I was sent to join this new work detail.

I was assigned to a mobile garage that travelled all around Estonia servicing and repairing German vehicles. We would move from camp to camp, repairing whatever vehicles had broken down before moving on. We would work all day, and at night we would sleep at the closest labour camp.

Each night we would sleep on the same bunks as the other prisoners. We also shared the same meals, which were very meagre. Each morning we would be given a ration of dark bread, about the size of a sandwich. I would break my portion in two, eat half for breakfast, and save one to eat before I went to sleep. I knew that I wouldn't be able to sleep with an empty stomach.

One morning, I got up and put my hands in the pocket of my coat to warm them, and found a little crumb of bread that had broken off the previous day. It was no larger than the tip of my finger, but I felt as though I had won the lotto. We did not get the nutrition we needed, nor enough calories to keep us alive for very long.

After the Germans ate each day, they would leave their scraps on the table, crusts of bread and so on, and once they left we would grab everything we could. There were seventeen Jewish boys on the labour detail in the garage, and we would carefully divide everything up between us. We understood that the only way we would survive was to look after each other.

That said, one time a driver in charge of one of the cars was so happy with my work he gave me a piece of chocolate. Just one little square, but it was the first time I'd had chocolate since I'd left my home in Vilna. I ate the whole thing, scoffed it down, didn't even think of sharing it with the other boys. There was no guilt—I knew I might not live very long, and this might be the last piece of chocolate I ever had.

–

We had to try to find the humour in all situations. In the absence of food, we sought whatever we could to sustain us, and naturally gravitated towards laughter as a counterweight to the depressing reality we were subjected to.

The giant depot trucks where the Germans kept the spare parts and machinery were always parked far away from the camps and other buildings, to avoid detection by aircraft.

Our guards discovered that one of the men on our work detail was a talented painter. They asked him to paint the depot truck to camouflage it, making it harder to spot from the air. He threw himself into the task, painting an intricate pattern of autumn leaves across the entire truck so that it blended seamlessly into the forest.

Then winter came. Somehow, the SS had not anticipated the change of season. Suddenly this truck with the lovely autumn-themed camouflage was glowing red, green and orange in the middle of a field of snow. A squad of SS officers arrived and were furious. They demanded to know who had painted the truck and wanted to shoot the man as a saboteur. He had to work hard to convince the Nazis not to shoot him.

'How was I supposed to know,' he objected, 'that the climate would change?'

It was very serious at the time, but after everyone had calmed down and put away their guns, it was very funny.

III

Every so often the garage would pack up and drive cross-country to service another camp. I ended up visiting several camps during the course of the war.

This gave me an opportunity to save the life of a friend, Izydor Zyskowicz, who everyone called Zis. I told the head of the garage I needed an assistant, and that Zis was a very talented auto-electrician. This was not entirely true. Zis was a terrible electrician, but he was a very good welder and learned to do new tasks quickly. Soon we were both indispensable to the garage and became very good companions working side by side.

At one point, the travelling garage returned to Kivioli, a camp I'd previously visited and which by then had grown into the largest hard labour camp in Estonia. There, one of the Jewish leaders had good news for me. He'd managed to obtain a prisoner manifest from camp Klooga, the easternmost labour camp in Estonia. My father's name was on it. You could not imagine my relief to find out he was still alive.

One day we were sent to a camp—Goldfilz—where I stayed for two nights. There, I met my old friend, the poet Hirsch Glick. He was still alive, and still writing poetry, carefully assembling each word in his head until the poems were perfect. Of course, in the camp he wasn't allowed pen or paper, so he carried them around in his head, hoping he would one day be free to record them.

Even in the camp, his poetry made him something of a celebrity. At mealtimes he was better treated than the other prisoners, and the cooks would give him a ladle of soup from the bottom of the cauldron which might contain a piece of potato.

It was very distressing to see this brilliant, sensitive man suffering such hardship, and I asked if there was anything I could do to help him.

'Can you get me a spoon?' he asked. The Germans provided prisoners with a metal dish of soup at mealtimes, but nothing to eat it with. You had to eat with your hands and lick the bowl clean. It was undignified, and in the poor hygiene of a prison camp, it was also dangerous.

I immediately fetched him a spoon I'd taken from the workshop, and sharpened one end so it could be used as a knife.

I gave it to him, and asked if there was anything else he needed. He told me: 'Only freedom. That is the most important thing for me.'

That was the last time I saw him. Years later I would meet a man, a Mr Samuel Drabkin, who told me that he was in the camp with Hirsch. One night, he said, while returning from work, Hirsch and his fellow prisoners, among them Samuel Drabkin and his four brothers, noticed that there was a hive of activity in the camp, and the Camp Commandant was drunk. Forty prisoners, including Hirsch, entered a toilet block, climbed through the window, broke through the camp's wire enclosure, jumped over the water ditch and escaped. Estonian guards fired at them, and of the forty escapees, only fourteen survived. Hirsch Glick did not make it. Mr Drabkin's brother saw him shot and killed. Strangely enough, different accounts of his death circulated far and wide after the war. The official version is that he escaped and joined an armed resistance group in the Estonian forest, and kept on fighting until finally dying in combat. It is natural for people to remember him in a heroic fashion, but regardless of how Hirsch was killed, I take some solace in knowing he did manage to escape, no matter how briefly, before they took his life.

IV

Like Hirsch, my greatest wish was to escape, and I was constantly on alert for opportunities to do so. That winter was very bitter. To get to work we had to walk through the snow fields. The snow was so thick you had to fight your way through it, so we walked in a single line. The Latvian SS officer in charge of us was very strict. He made us walk as a unit, singing a song in Russian so that we couldn't talk among ourselves.

One day, we were returning from work when a terrible storm blew in. The wind was howling and the snow was so heavy that visibility was down to almost nothing. The Latvian SS started shouting for us to stay close, that he would lead us back to camp. I realised this was an opportunity to escape.

I knew that there was a little Estonian village just a few kilometres away. If I could slip away in the blizzard, I could make it there. I ran off, and stumbled through the snow until I came to a little cottage, still some distance outside the village. I knocked on the door, and a middle-aged woman answered it. The moment she saw me she knew exactly where I'd come from.

'You must be hungry,' she said to me. That was her only comment. She asked no questions, just invited me in and gave me the biggest meal I'd ever eaten in my life. I drank two whole bottles of milk, and ate two loaves of bread and a tin of preserved fish. I stayed there until the storm subsided enough for me to leave. As I left, she told me to come back anytime, promising there would be a meal waiting for me. I was very grateful, but I never planned to return. I was going to escape.

I walked off and realised that I was free. All I had to do was start running—I could leave the camp behind forever and find my way to safety. It was an ecstatic feeling, the most joy I'd experienced in many months. My excitement drove me onwards through the snow until I reached a fork in the road and realised I faced a dilemma. To the left was the road leading back to the camp. If I went right, it would take me to the village, and the world beyond that. But how far could I possibly I make it? It was a freezing winter night. I had no food, inadequate clothing, and there was a good chance that the first human being I met on the road would denounce me and take me back to the camp. If that happened, I would be severely punished. It was an impossible choice, but in the end, I turned left, back to the camp.

The guard at the gate was the Latvian SS officer who'd been escorting us. He looked furious.

'Where have you been?' he said, staring at me suspiciously.

'I got lost in the storm and had to take shelter,' I said. 'But I'm loyal to the camp, so I came back the moment I could.'

The Latvian was unconvinced. When I left I'd been so weak I could barely walk through the snow. Now, after a meal, my cheeks were swollen and colour had come back to my complexion.

'Tell me the truth,' he said.

So I confessed, and told him that I'd stumbled upon a woman who'd been kind enough to shelter and feed me.

Further, she'd promised to feed me any time I knocked on her door. The Latvian thought about this for a while, then unexpectedly said, 'I'm on guard every Thursday between eight and ten. If you give me your word of honour to come back, I'll let you out to visit her then.'

So for the next three weeks, each Thursday I would slip out past the guard, sneak in the back door of the woman's house and have a huge meal, then race back to the camp before any of the other guards noticed me gone. It was wonderful, until the third visit, when I entered the back door and froze in horror. Outside I could hear the bells of a horse-drawn carriage approaching. The woman and I stared at each other, our eyes wide, as the bells drew closer. The poor woman was so terrified her face drained of all colour. The bells stopped outside her house, and I ran.

Moving quietly, I sneaked through her garden. I was worried that someone would follow my tracks, so I spent a half hour going in circles, crossing the road again and again to confuse any pursuers. I never went back there—as hungry as I was, it wasn't worth putting the poor woman's life at risk.

I still went out at night whenever that Latvian SS gave me the opportunity. There were many farmhouses in the area surrounding the camp. I would go from door to door to beg for scraps.

When a new prisoner arrived at a camp they were given a blanket. Because so many of us were dying so quickly, there was soon a surplus of blankets. There were piles of them, each so badly infested with lice that they began to change colour. They really weren't suitable for an animal, let alone a human being. But in them I saw an opportunity.

Whenever I could leave the camp, I would put a blanket over my arm and visit a neighbouring farmhouse, where I would ask them if they wanted to buy a blanket for their horse. Some would slam the door in my face, but most would give me a little food. Whatever I had, I would take back and share with my friends.

One farmer didn't shut the door on me; he left it open while he went to fetch a piece of bread. Through the door I could see into the kitchen of the house, where a young girl was sitting at the table, reading a book and eating biscuits.

That image stayed with me for maybe six months. Such a simple scene to think of now, more than half a century later, but at the time, in my half-starved, half-mad mind, I thought I'd seen through into heaven. I could not imagine that such a place existed on the same Earth as the reality I was enduring.

Every night when I was falling asleep, I would fantasise

that I was at that table, sitting by the fire, reading a book, eating a biscuit.

Every scrap of food, every calorie one could get one's hands on was important. Perhaps even more so were the little moments of hope that kept us going.

I may not have survived if it weren't for the Latvian SS officer who looked the other way when I went out in the evenings to forage for food from houses in the village. I got the best results from knocking on the doors of farmers. Sometimes they had a piece of bread or two they would share with me.

When I told Zis about this, he said he wanted to come with me, and I convinced the guard to let him out. So out we went. Zis was two years older than me, twenty-four to my twenty-two, and those two years made a huge difference—he was much, much smarter about survival than I was. I told Zis that I wanted to try to beg at a farmhouse.

'Don't be stupid!' he told me. 'Let's go to the village and find a rich man. Then we'll get more than a piece of bread!'

So we found our way to the village square, where all the grandest houses were. Sure enough, right on the edge of the square was a very prominent house, almost a mansion. We ran up and knocked at the door. When it swung open, standing there in the doorframe, with a huge smile on his face, was an Estonian SS officer, in full uniform with a pistol in his belt.

'Hello children!' he said. 'How nice of you to visit. It's my job to hunt you down when you go missing, and here you come and knock at my door and save me some time.'

I thought that surely this was it, the last moment of my life, but Zis was already thinking fast.

'I'm a welder,' he said. 'A friend of yours told me you've got some farm equipment that needs repair. How can I help?'

The SS officer was unconvinced. 'Who sent you?'

'Kaspar,' said Zis.

'I don't know any Kaspar.'

'Oh, I meant Maksim, or maybe it was Rasmus . . .' Zis proceeded to list every Estonian name he could think of, getting through six or seven before the officer cut him off.

'Do you mean Ivan?' he said.

'Oh yes, Ivan!' said Zis. 'How could I forget?

It turned out that Zis was the best possible man for this situation. Not only could he talk his way out of anything, but this SS officer happened to need a welder badly. The Germans had confiscated all the welding equipment in the town for their own use. For the next three weeks, every Thursday night Zis would visit the SS man, pick up a piece of machinery for repair, and take it back to our garage to work on it. I was convinced that the day he finished all the work he would be shot, but in the end the SS officer gave him some food and sent him back to camp.

I never took Zis out with me again, and stuck to visiting farmhouses on my own. But he did come with me when the garage travelled on to the next camp. In time, I learned to joke about it.

The Germans in charge of the garage were decent people. Although they worked for the Nazis, these men treated the prisoners who worked with them like human beings.

We were not allowed access to news; not the radio, not the newspaper. I craved the simple pleasure of being able to read a newspaper, but we were forbidden to touch them. One of the mechanics let me read the newspaper over his shoulder, by putting it on the bench and slowly turning the pages as I finished reading them. I can't tell you how happy I was just to stand there, reading the pages of a real-life newspaper.

When Christmas arrived that year, another German mechanic was sent a cake, one of those traditional spiced fruit cakes, and he called me over and cut a piece for me. Just a small piece, but that was the greatest gift I could imagine. It wasn't that I'd been given some extra food, it was that I was being treated like a human being.

On one occasion a driver came in with a jeep-style open car for repair. He'd been driving it in the rain, and the water that pooled at the bottom of the car had already turned to ice. To get at the electrical components under the floor I had to chip away at the ice. I removed a large sheet of ice, and found, hidden safely beneath it, a bottle of beer. I couldn't believe it. Nor could I resist it.

A few minutes after I had finished it, the driver returned, looked around his car, and turned to me.

'Did you see a bottle of beer just now?'

'I don't know anything about that,' I said. He looked at me, very unconvinced. I smelled strongly of beer, and was lightheaded—it was my first beer in a long time, and I had drunk it on a very empty stomach. He knew exactly what had happened, but he wasn't angry.

'Why are you in a labour camp?' he asked. 'What did you do?'

'I am Jewish. I haven't done anything.'

'You don't look Jewish,' he said. 'Why don't you have a Jewish nose?'

I assured him that I was Jewish, that Jewish people have all different kinds of noses and, in fact, look just like regular people, because we were.

He walked away, and I waited for the guards to come for me. It never happened; the man didn't report my theft. He was a decent fellow, a human being, just like me. He was just a victim of propaganda, like so many who had been tricked into hatred all across Europe.

V

All things considered, I was in a relatively fortunate situation compared to many other Jews. Initially, I was allowed to keep my civilian clothes, which was an incredible blessing. When I was first taken to the labour camp, I was fortunate enough to be wearing my best suit—well-tailored, warm and crafted from imported English material. At night, when I went to bed, I would remove it and carefully fold it up so that it didn't crease. If I found a way to escape, I wanted to be able to pass as a civilian, not a fugitive from a labour camp.

Even more important were my boots, the French army ones my father had acquired for me in the Ghetto. They were still a little too big for me, so I filled the space between my feet and the leather with rags. Underneath those rags, I hid precious photographs of my family.

These boots were priceless to me. Each day we had to walk in the snow, and the wooden clogs our captors supplied were of little use. The snow would soak into the wood, and the clogs would grow so heavy it became impossible to keep trudging. Often people would just collapse where they stood because they couldn't take another step.

My boots kept me alive day after day through the brutal winter. I was so afraid of losing them that at night I would use them as a pillow, and stay awake as long as I could, in case someone tried to steal them.

Every day I was a little bit thinner, and a little bit weaker. One day, I arrived to work at the garage and collapsed. The commander realised I couldn't work, and sent me to the barracks within the camp that was used as a makeshift hospital. By the time I arrived, I was delirious, with a very high temperature. The triage station consisted of several crude mattresses; burlap sacks stuffed with straw, lined up on the floor. I lay down to sleep, and later woke to the Nazi commander standing in the door, screaming at me. 'You lazy people! I know you aren't sick, I know you're pretending you are ill to get off work!'

I rose up from my mattress and started to walk towards him. He must have realised then that there was something really wrong with me, as he turned pale, backed away, and ran off in a hurry. I lay back down and didn't move for two weeks.

It was typhoid. I was already terribly weak and knew my chances of survival were not good. The days and nights blurred into each other, and I would slip between fevered dreams and my waking nightmare. Other sick men lay on either side of me, thrashing in their own delirium. Often they would collapse on top of me and I would be too weak to push them off.

My friends from the garage came to visit me, and I decided to give them my clothes, figuring I would not be needing them anymore. I divided them up equally between my friends—one fellow got the trousers, one the shirt, one the coat. I gave my precious French army boots to my best friend, Zis Zyskowicz.

After they left, I began to contemplate my situation. I knew that even if I survived my sickness, I probably would not recover. If I walked out of the hospital barracks, it would be as a *muselmann*, one of the prisoners who were so badly starved they had become walking skeletons. I'd seen what happens to a man at that stage: the eyes go dead, they can think only about finding a scrap of bread. They lose their dignity, and with it the will to live. I did not want to be one of them. I would rather die.

It took me some effort but, crawling on my hands and knees, I made it outside, where I lay down in the snow and waited for the cold to finish me off. It was no good. The snow was−20 degrees, but my temperature was 40 degrees, so the snow simply melted away as I lay on it. After a couple of hours, still alive, I gave up on the idea and crawled back to my straw mattress.

That night the prisoners lying on either side both flung their feet across me. They had died in the night of complications from typhoid, and were now just two dead bodies pinning me to the bed. I was too weak to move; all I could do was wait until the morning, when a nurse came to take the bodies away.

When that happened, a small miracle occurred. The nurse came and looked at me, and then she opened my mouth and put a few drops of milk on my tongue. It was the only food I'd been able to keep down since I fell ill. After that night, I started to recover. I'm not sure if it was the snow that brought my fever down, or that small act of kindness from the nurse, but my temperature began to fall, and I got a little stronger.

That same day, they sent me back to camp, dressed in trousers that were so long I had to roll them up to the knee. I had my first meal in ages, and began to track down my friends so I could reclaim my possessions. All of them were happy to give them back, except the fellow I had given my trousers too. It took Zis persuading him before I got them back.

I was still not at all well the next day when I went back to work. The foreman asked me to remove the generator from a car and recondition it. It was a simple job, one I'd done dozens of times, but I could not understand what he was saying. I could remember the word 'generator', but no matter how hard I tried, I couldn't match any meaning to it in my head. The foreman saw that I was not functioning properly, and took me from the garage to a secluded room in the mechanics' living quarters.

He directed me to lay down on the floor next to a power point in the wall, then put a screwdriver in my hand.

'Rest now,' he told me. 'If somebody comes in, tell them you are repairing this power point.' In the evening, when the truck came to take us back to the labour camp, he made sure I stood in the middle of the truck, with men on either side of me, so I wouldn't fall off. For three days, he repeated this scene, and let me rest all day in a warm room. He saved my life.

VI

The SS would regularly perform what they called 'selections'. All the prisoners would line up in neat columns, and camp doctors would inspect each one. Those who were weak, or too sick to stand, or recovering from a beating would be 'selected' and loaded onto a truck. Before they left, one of the SS officers would give a brief speech, telling them they would be moved to a new camp, one specifically to allow for rest and recovery. There they would enjoy ample food and sleep until they were well enough to work again.

Those selected believed they were being told the truth. In total, 400 men were selected. The sick and wounded prisoners climbed onto transport trucks, overjoyed at the prospect of food and rest. We watched, knowing they were going to be executed, driven into the forest and shot.

On most Sundays the mines, workshops and garages where the labour camp inmates worked shut down. On these days, rather than let us rest, they took us to the field next to the camp and told us to carry rocks from one side of the field to the other. When the entire pile had been moved across the field, we were instructed to move it back. It was meaningless, humiliating and exhausting, but that was the point. The Nazi policy was to work us to the bone, denying us rest and solidarity, and ultimately robbing us of the will to rebel. The Germans were very methodical in everything they did, even when it seemed to make no sense. Each Sunday when we had to carry rocks, we stopped for a break at precisely twelve o'clock. The whistle would go off, and we would lie on the ground and try to rest. Just because our treatment was insane was no excuse not to be punctual!

We were so hungry; all we would ever talk about was food. Each day me and four friends would sit on the ground and eat the scraps we were given and reminisce about foods we had once eaten. A man could sit and talk poetically about the way his mother had prepared fried bread and potato dumplings until we were all half-mad with hunger.

I remember one day we got an even smaller ration than usual: three potatoes for all five of us. My friends trusted me to be fair, so I had to divide it up, and naturally I ended up with the smallest piece. It was gone in one mouthful.

'You know none of us are going to survive this,' one of the men said. 'We are going to die here.'

Days like that made it very hard to keep up hope. It was like walking through a dark tunnel towards a light that never got any closer, no matter how far we walked. The distance to freedom seemed impossibly far. But still, we could not let go of that light. We had to find a way to keep going.

'Let's make a promise,' I said. 'We must survive, even if it's just for five minutes of freedom. If any of us make it, we will tell the world what the Germans did. We will hold them responsible for all of this.'

We all promised, and shook on it. We would find a way to live through this. We would tell the world what had happened. We would not be forgotten.

4

Two Steps Forward

I

BY LATE 1943, IT SEEMED CERTAIN TO ME THAT THE Germans would lose the war. It was the only logical outcome. It gave me some hope, knowing that if I could hold on a little longer, I might be liberated from all of this.

The Soviets controlled the skies over Estonia. Russian planes would patrol the roads we used to move from camp to camp, firing at anything that moved.

The planes would appear out of the overcast winter sky, flying so low that they were just above the treetops, and rake the German caravans with machine gunfire. One time we were marching back from work, exhausted, and suddenly heard the roar of a plane above us. I threw myself down in the thick snow and covered my head. I could see little puffs of snow being thrown up where the high-calibre rounds were hitting the ground. They came racing towards me and then passed me by, just a few feet away from my head. Luckily this particular pilot wasn't a very good shot!

The Germans realised they needed to find a way to protect themselves from the relentless Soviet air attacks. They assembled a network of barrage balloons—huge balloons tethered to steel cables that posed a deadly obstacle to any plane flying overhead, particularly in the poor visibility of an Estonian winter.

One day the balloon barrier downed a Soviet aircraft, and it crashed into a nearby field. At first the German army were jubilant—they'd taken out one of the Russian pilots that had been picking them off for weeks—but their joy turned to despair when they found the plane and began dismantling it for parts. They discovered that the ball-bearings in the plane were manufactured in America, which meant that the Americans were assisting the Soviet war effort. American industry and Soviet bravery were not a combination the Germans wanted to face on the battlefield.

The German armed forces were already depleted. They were running out of soldiers, ordnance, fuel and spare parts for their tanks and aeroplanes.

Because I had the ability to repair vehicles and recycle old and worn-out parts, I became more and more valuable as a prisoner the longer the war went on. My specific skill provided the answer to mechanical problems that

German engineers had not foreseen when they brought their machinery to Estonia.

For example, the backbone of Nazi logistics was the fleet of trucks they used to transport troops, equipment, ammunition and provisions across their occupied territories. These trucks were absolutely enormous, more than four tonnes, and very well made. As beautifully manufactured as these engines were, they had not been designed with the Northern European winter in mind. They had one fatal design flaw: the starter motor.

The starter motor is one of the most important electrical systems in an auto-engine. When the driver turns a vehicle's ignition switch, this brings two electrical relays into contact, completing an electrical circuit which then causes the engine to turn over and the vehicle to begin burning petrol.

In the extreme cold of the Estonian winter, the starter motor did not have enough magnetic force to bring the relay points together, and so the trucks would not start.

Due in part to my self-taught education, I was able to figure out a way to repair all these disabled trucks. I knew that the climate would be affecting the strength of the magnetic field. The solution was as simple as removing the starter motor and making the gap in the relay smaller, so that even in the freezing cold the two points could come into contact.

It took me no longer than three hours to repair a truck in this way, and in doing so, I solved a major headache for the Germans. Previously, they'd had to burn precious oil on a tray underneath the sump to keep it warm enough so that the truck would start in the morning. From there, the one functional truck would have to tow the others around in an attempt to warm them up.

My method was much simpler and saved a great deal of oil and petrol. The foremen were delighted with my work. I was very happy with it as well, but for a different reason.

I knew that the repair would not last very long. When retuning the mechanism, I was very careful to make the gap between the two relay points just a little too small. When the engine had been running for a while and started to warm up, the magnets in the terminals would cause them to snap together and fuse, which would burn the starter motor out and cripple the vehicle.

Importantly, this would not happen until the truck was some distance away from the garage, deep in Estonian territory. It was my hope that the trucks would then be easy targets for Russian aircraft or Estonian partisans. With this small act of sabotage, I could do my part to resist, even while trapped in a labour camp.

Luckily, the Nazis never suspected that I was behind the trucks breaking down out in the wilderness. If they had, I would have been executed without delay. As it happened, the Germans were extremely grateful for the solution I presented, and held me in great esteem, even rewarding me with a little extra food whenever I rescued a truck from the scrap heap. They needed every vehicle they could keep on the road. The situation for the Germans was getting worse and worse.

At this stage in the war, the Soviet frontline was not far away from us. The giant German truck that held all the spare parts necessary to sustain the war effort was hidden in the forest in the Gulf of Finland. Across the water, the Soviet troops were massing.

One night, in a clandestine operation, Soviet saboteurs crossed the water and robbed the truck. They stole everything: machine parts, tools, even the heating elements used to warm the insides of the truck.

After that, we had to work in terribly frigid conditions. The cold was so extreme that if I arrived at the truck first thing in the morning and picked up a spanner, it would freeze to my hand. Conditions were terrible, and Soviet planes were coming more and more frequently. The Germans made the decision to withdraw, abandoning all their installations. This also meant moving the prisoners they used for forced labour to camps even deeper in German territory.

II

The Germans evacuated the camps, loading all prisoners onto transport trucks. I saw a man named Foster, one of the Germans who worked with me in the garage, watch my friends being herded onto the truck. He turned away with tears in his eyes. He knew that he would never see them again, and assumed that they would not live much longer. I will never forget Foster's tears. He was a decent man, despite the circumstances that threw us together.

Our destination was the seaport called Revel, in the city of Tallinn, about half a day's drive away. I was assigned to travel on the giant German truck containing the mobile workshop, a more comfortable trip than many of my fellow prisoners experienced.

From my perch on the truck I could see the devastation the war had wrought on Estonia, and the terrible state the German army was in. We drove through swamps where the roads were lined with dead and injured German soldiers. Some of them had the strength to call out as we passed:

'Help me! Please help me!'

From my comfortable position on the truck, I waved back cheerfully and yelled, 'Not today!'

That was an extremely pleasant feeling, to see the army that had murdered so many of my friends brought so low.

Despite the propaganda in the newspapers and on the radio, it was clear that the Germans were losing the war.

The truck stopped for a break close to a German field hospital, and I decided to go inside. Nobody stopped me—there were too few staff to do so. The hospital was overwhelmed with wounded soldiers and there were not enough medics or nurses to provide basic care. I came across a ward with six soldiers lying in bed, all comatose, each with a loaf of bread placed on the floor by their head.

Behind the hospital was a kitchen where cooks were preparing rich meals for the soldiers. It was a waste—none of the soldiers in the hospital could stomach the food. It would be thrown out if I didn't eat it.

I took the opportunity to feast, enjoying a huge meal rich with carbohydrates and meat. I don't know how I didn't get sick from it, but I managed to keep it all down. When I left, I returned to the ward of comatose soldiers and took one loaf of bread for myself, and one for my father. I assumed that if I were being evacuated, so too was my father, and we would eventually end up in the same place.

From the field hospital we walked to the port, where a transport ship was waiting for us. One of the SS officers in charge gave a speech. We were used to SS men screaming at us and inflicting humiliation and violence. This man was very polite and spoke reasonably, thanking us for our service.

'You men have worked very hard for the Reich, and the German State thanks you for it. You have our gratitude. Now, because you need rest, it is time for you to recover.' He told us that we were to board the boat, where we would be taken to another camp to recuperate. There, as a reward for our labour, we could rest, and enjoy good food.

Would you believe it, I thought he was telling the truth. Although I had seen many people told this same lie after selections, had seen my friends driven away to their deaths, somehow, in my malnourished, desperate state, I was willing to believe the SS officer. It is very strange. Perhaps it is part of human nature, to gravitate towards hope to the point where we will believe a comfortable lie when the reality is so hopeless.

We were at sea for seven days as we sailed from Revel to Danzig, a German port on the Baltic sea near the border of Germany and Poland. They fed us adequately—still starvation rations, but an absolutely luxurious amount of food after the deprivations we had suffered. The sun was shining, the weather warm enough that we could sleep out under the stars on the deck of the boat. We would lay down for the night and SS men would walk around checking that we were comfortable. For those few days, we experienced a kind of freedom, and for that brief moment in time, I truly believed that the war was over, that we had been liberated.

When we arrived at Danzig, our 'holiday' was over, and reality returned. We were ordered to march to a new concentration camp—Stutthof.

It was two days hard march, with no food or water. On the second day of marching, we were ordered to sit down and take a rest. I was sitting on the side of the road, on a patch of sandy, gritty ground when I noticed something wonderful. Scattered through the dirt and pebbles were little crumbs of bread; someone had sat here previously and eaten their lunch, leaving food behind. I couldn't believe my luck.

Quickly, before anyone else noticed, I began to shovel the dirt into my mouth, trying to swallow the bread and spit out the rocks. I was delirious with hunger, but the meal of dirt and stones did not help much. It caused me a great deal of trouble later on, when the dirt I swallowed caused me to develop kidney stones. In time, that desperate snack would put me in hospital.

III

On the march to Stutthof, we were joined by some Kapos from the camp. Kapos were camp prisoners who the Nazis had chosen as guards for the rest of the prisoners. They were hand-picked by the SS, often from violent criminal gangs rather than the ranks of political prisoners, and were known for their brutality and cruelty against their fellow inmates. In a system designed to turn victim against victim, Kapos did the dirty work of the SS for them. Without them, there could be no concentration camps, but with their help, a handful of SS could keep control over vast numbers of prisoners. These Kapos now taunted us, saying that we were being marched to our death. One of them described in great detail the Nazi gas chambers, where prisoners who had been selected to die would be cruelly tricked and brutally executed en masse. Men, women and children would be told they were being given the opportunity to shower, and thrown into a tiled room lined with shower heads. But no water would come from those pipes—instead, a canister of poison gas, Zyklon-B, would be dropped into the room. The gas would kill every-one within twenty minutes. A horrible way to die.

Stutthof was one of the first concentration camps built outside of German borders in World War II, and by the time I arrived at the end of July 1944, all pretence of civility had been abandoned. Conditions were so harsh that thou-sands of Jews, Poles and other political prisoners were dying from starvation, extreme labour conditions and lack of medical care. This was not fast enough for Hitler's 'Final Solution', however, and the SS were murdering Jews as fast as they could: with guns, batons, gas, and by any brutal means they could think of.

On our arrival, Kapos were waiting to process us. They stripped us naked and sprayed us with disinfectant, then pointed to a building about 500 metres away and told us to run there. There were SS men on both sides with ferocious dogs, which would maul us if we stopped moving.

'Do you think they will gas us?' my friend asked me. 'Are we walking towards a gas chamber?'

'No, I don't think so. Why would they have disinfected us if they were about to gas us?' I tried to think logically about it, although I did not have much hope myself. It seemed to me a certainty that this was the moment when I would die. I believed this right up until I stood under the shower and the tap started spraying water down on us. The relief was unbelievable. A shower is always nice, but as you can imagine, I was particularly pleased to find myself in this one.

I left the shower, still naked, shivering in the cold. That's when I learned I would not be getting my clothes back. The Kapos took all of our belongings, including our clothes. Instead, I received a mismatched combination of a short shirt, long trousers and a short woman's coat. You were given clothes selected at random, so nobody's clothes fitted them properly.

This was not just carelessness on behalf on the Germans, it was deliberate provocation, designed to humiliate and degrade our morale.

Everything the Nazis did to make me feel inferior only made me more convinced that my humanity was stronger. Nothing they could do would make me ethically inferior to the people who imprisoned and humiliated us. This was of utmost importance. The only effective weapon we had against the Holocaust was to retain our decency.

They took my boots, and with them I lost the treasured photos of my family, hidden under the rags inside the toes.

My precious boots were replaced with a very old pair, several sizes too large for me with the sole worn through. As if that wasn't bad enough, the first time I was taken for an exercise, I saw another Jew wearing my boots.

'Look, excuse me,' I said, approaching him. 'Those are my boots. Would you mind if I have them back?'

He responded: 'They were your boots yesterday. Today they are my boots.'

I tried appealing to his sense of decency.

'Imagine you were me,' I said. 'If you saw someone wearing your boots, wouldn't you want them to return them to you? Is that not what a decent person would do? Now you have a chance to be a good person.'

'Yes, I suppose so,' he agreed, and gave me back the boots. You can't image my sense of triumph. It may not sound like much, but getting those boots back was one of the most important achievements of my life.

When we first arrived at Stutthof, there were no quarters to house us, so they put us into Barrack No. 10. This was a barrack especially constructed to house SS men. There were marble floors, beautiful bathrooms and comfortable beds—enough of them that we could sleep two to a bed. It might have been very comfortable, but the SS made sure that we didn't enjoy it much. There was a guard at the door at night who hated having to let us out to go to the bathroom. He would beat you when you left to walk to the toilet, and beat you again on your return.

We had one particularly cruel Kapo who would make us lie down on the cement floor in front of the barracks and spray freezing water over us, so that we would go to bed soaked and shiver all night long.

One of the young SS men would take us into the forest to harvest firewood. While we were busy picking up branches, he would sneak up behind us with his baton and strike us across the legs. He liked to hear us scream, and would hit us again and again until we screamed in pain.

I never screamed. The moment I realised what he wanted from me, I knew I would never give it to him. He kept coming back and hitting me harder and harder, but with each blow, my resolve strengthened. I think he would have killed me, had he not grown tired and bored and moved on to the next Jew.

One day we were instructed to move a cart full of dried onion from one location in the camp to another. We were allowed to eat as many onions as we could stomach, and I hid some of them up my sleeve. The next day, when I went to work, the Kapo said that he could smell the onion, and started beating me mercilessly. Not far away, a young Jewish girl was working, and she screamed out in horror.

'Stop hurting him!' she cried. 'That's my brother!'

I had never seen that girl before, but her quick thinking saved my life. The Kapo stopped beating me, and as punishment sent me on a work detail where they gave me the job of separating good potatoes from bad. As it happens, when you are as hungry as I was there are no potatoes you judge to be bad, so I had no labour to do, and could rest and recover from my beating.

That kind stranger was not my sister, and I missed my sister terribly. I had lost the precious photo I had of her when the Nazis took away my boots. Unfortunately, by the time I got them back, the photos of my family had been found and destroyed. That was a terrible blow to my morale, but as it turned out, my family was closer than I imagined.

I only found this out years later, but Maria Grodnizka had been interned in Stutthof at the same time as me—along with my sister Bella! They were classified as Polish political prisoners, while I was in another section for Jewish prisoners, so our paths never crossed.

Bella had survived since our separation, and had been living free for much of the war. She and Maria had been able to escape the liquidation of the Ghetto and to live for a time with their false Aryan papers. Civilians living on Aryan papers in occupied Lithuania were required to report to the police station each month to have their documents stamped. The underground had made a counterfeit stamp so that those living on false papers could have their documents certified without risking detection.

Unfortunately, the Germans discovered this underground facility, and were waiting on the day Maria and Bella came to get their papers stamped. They were arrested as suspected members of the Polish underground and sent to Stutthof.

Bella had become very weak in Stutthof—too weak to eat anymore. Maria had to chew her bread for her, then put it into Bella's mouth. This was the only way to keep her alive. Were it not for Maria, she would have perished there.

In the end, I was only in Stutthof for a few weeks, until the former prisoners of the Estonian labour camps were summoned to a special project in the south of Germany.

Before they gave up on their desperate plan to mine shale-oil, the Nazis would stage a last-ditch effort to

make the technology work in Bavaria. They had discovered oil-rich shale rock in Southern Germany's Baden
Württemburg region, at a place called Dautmergen, one of
the sub-camps of the Natzweiler-Struthof concentration
complex. They needed forced labourers with experience
in shale-rock mining, and so veterans of Estonian labour
camps were transported to Dautmergen.

IV

They transported us in train wagons. We didn't get any
food or water for the length of the trip—about two days.
Whenever we stopped at a station, the Nazis would open
the door so we could clearly see the fountains bubbling
away in the train station courtyards. We were terribly
thirsty—one man jumped off the train to try to reach a
fountain and get a drink, and was immediately shot.

The train did not take us all the way to Dautmergen,
as the rails did not reach that far. We had to disembark
and walk the rest of the way, about an hour's walk though
farmland.

It was autumn, and the path took us straight through an
orchard. Fruit trees lined the road. Apples and pears, left
to ripen on the branches so they could be made into cider,
hung all around us, close enough for us to touch.

We were warned not to try and take any—one man who reached for a piece of fruit on the ground was shot in the arm. This was as good as being shot dead—his death would just come more slowly. If you could not work, the Nazis had no reason to let you live another day. So, we walked on, the ripe fruit on the ground being crushed under our feet.

As we walked, the ground underfoot turned from farmland to swamp. Dautmergen was a very small camp that had been forced to rapidly expand to accommodate the shale-mining operation.

The conditions in this camp were particularly miserable. The entire facility was built on a swamp, so everything was always wet. The damp got into everything—our clothes, our beds. It was something of a unique camp, in that we were kept under control by Nazi soldiers. Perhaps they didn't trust Kapos to run this particular facility.

My job was to carry bags of cement and rails across to the site where they were building a narrow-gauge railway into the swamp to make mining more efficient. The bags weighed twenty kilograms each, and I was already so weak from hunger I could barely lift them. If I were to stumble and fall, or drop a bag, I would be shot on sight.

On my first night at Dautmergen I lay on the bed and wondered if I would be able to get up in the morning. Already exhausted, I knew that I could not handle this labour for long. I would last a day, maybe a week if I were lucky, before I could no longer rise from the bed and would therefore be executed. It would have been easy for me to give up and pass away in the night, but the possibility of getting a bowl of coffee and a piece of bread in the morning was so enticing that I could not stand to let myself die before I ate again. The hunger was so all-consuming that it took priority over death!

Each morning we would be woken before six o'clock by a screaming German guard. We would be given a bowl of warm brown liquid they rather optimistically called 'coffee' and a scrap of bread.

Then we would all line up, standing in neat rows while they counted us to check that nobody had escaped during the night. As there were thousands of us, this took a great deal of time. If the guards got distracted, or lost count, they would simply start again, and we would be forced to stand still in the swamp until the guards were satisfied.

It was freezing cold, often raining, and we were usually soaked through. All around us people would collapse and perish from exposure and exhaustion. In some ways, this was one of the most traumatic experiences that I can recall: this senseless, orderly cruelty; the same every morning. It is horrifying to stand still in the rain, waiting for a bureaucrat to count you off a list, while all around you your friends are collapsing. It is not a scene you often see in movies about the Holocaust. It does not capture the imagination of those who write fiction and make movies in the way the horror of the gas chamber and the crematorium does. But to live through, it was a nightmare, one that came to life each day. Every morning this would happen. The dreadful predictability of it was unnerving, and the cumulative stress began to erode even the strongest willed among us. The hard labour began before dawn and lasted all through the day, as we built the foundation of the future oil-mining site in a barren, frozen swamp.

On that first day, when the labour stopped, I lay down and let my tired hands sink into the snow. It was already spring, and beneath the snow, grass was starting to grow. I was so hungry that I began to clear away the snow and pull up handfuls of grass to chew on. By chance, at that moment the wind picked up and blew a piece of newspaper against my boot. Reaching down, I picked it up and smoothed it out, and I saw that it was a recipe for a cake. I read it closely, and closed my eyes, and for half an hour allowed myself to imagine that I was eating that cake. My hunger was so great that I could genuinely taste the soft, buttery cake and sweet, sweet icing with every mouthful of grass I swallowed.

That might sound as though I was going crazy, but I believe that moments like these were a very important factor in surviving the Holocaust. The physical trials, the starvation and beatings were not the only problems. The mental state, the psychological mindset with which you faced each day was just as important. If you could derive happiness from small moments—an act of kindness from a guard, a joke with a friend while you marched in the rain, a brief pastry-related hallucination while enjoying a snack of grass and dirt—these small things gave you a better chance of survival.

V

I made it through a week at Dautmergen, then another, and then I got very lucky. My friend Zis got a job in the garage in the nearest town, Balingen. Somehow, some other friends of mine got jobs in the garage too, and convinced them to take me on as an auto-electrician. So, I was relieved from the gruelling hard labour of carrying cement bags through the swamp.

Not long after that, I was rescued from the misery of Dautmergen, too. On one particularly wet and miserable morning, we had an especially deadly roll call. On this day, the Nazi officer in charge kept losing count. Then someone in the lines would succumb to exposure and collapse, and so the officer would have to start again. In the end, he counted us for four hours, well past the time we were meant to be at work. The foreman of the garage turned up looking for his workers and was appalled by the conditions at Dautmergen. He demanded that we be transferred to a different camp.

The new work detail was in Frommer, an even smaller sub-camp. It was about four kilometres away from Dautmergen, but it may as well have been a different planet.

The German mechanics who ran the garage in Balingen knew that the war was lost. They were deathly afraid of being sent to the front, and so pretended to be conducting research, claiming to be on the verge of perfecting a petrol engine to run on diesel fuel. This was impossible, as they well knew, but they invented an elaborate body of fake data that kept German command from mobilising them.

Now and again, someone would come from Berlin, an SS man who had been sent to check on the research. On that day, the German mechanics would yell and scream at the prisoners and threaten us. Then the SS would go home, and everyone would be polite again.

The man in charge was a Frenchman, a very decent fellow. This camp was still a prison, but compared to Dautmergen it was paradise. The Frenchman made sure we had proper rations of food, and we were even given rations of cigarettes. I didn't smoke, but I could trade them for things I needed. Seven cigarettes were enough to pay a shoemaker to repair the bottom of my boots.

In our work unit, there were only twelve Jews. I was working alongside prisoners from all sorts of groups who the Nazis had deemed criminal. Generally, the prisoners were French, Dutch, Belgians and German nationals who had mainly been imprisoned for political crimes.

Most importantly, the French commander went out of his way to keep our morale up. He had a clandestine radio, and every week on Sunday he would tune into the latest broadcasts from the BBC and update us with the news that the Germans were losing the war.

We learned that the Allied forces had all but overwhelmed the Germans. At night, we would hear the drone of British planes far overhead, which was like music to our ears.

To confuse the German radar, these planes would fire off 'chaff'—aluminium strips that would overwhelm radar signals with false echoes. Each morning we would emerge from the barracks and find the camp littered with little strips of aluminium, sparkling like snow. Those ugly strips of metal were a beautiful sight—they let us know we weren't alone, that help was on the way.

It wasn't long before the Americans started bombing during the daytime—military positions, houses, whatever caught their eye. Nobody could keep them from indiscriminately raining bombs on Germany. The Nazi opposition was shattered.

VI

In April 1945, Nazi soldiers shut down the Frommer concentration camp and told us we would be marched to yet another camp even deeper in German territory. We marched in columns, walking at night to avoid air attack. American bombers ruled the skies and would attack anything that moved. From the air, thousands of prisoners marching in formation looks very much like a battalion.

To hide us during the days, the Germans would find a barn somewhere on a farm and lock us in until night fell. Each day we would lie on the straw, wondering if the Germans would simply burn the building down and be done with us.

The nights were bitterly cold, and at that time of the year, it would rain steadily through the evenings, so we were dripping wet as we walked.

It did not take much to provoke the Germans to kill us. If we became too weak to keep walking, their response was a bullet. One fellow, Williams—very tall, once as strong as an ox—became too weak to take another step. He collapsed at the rear of the column one day. We tried to pick him up, but he was too heavy, and we were forced to keep walking ahead. A little way down the road, we heard a gunshot ring out, and surmised that an SS had remained behind to finish him off.

So, we kept marching. The guards were in bad shape. At this stage of the war, the German state was devastated in every way: economically, culturally, morally. Nearly every man old enough to hold a rifle had been sent to the frontlines, and many of them had never come back. The only men left to guard us on the death march were in their fifties and sixties, and they were not strong enough for the task. They could not even carry all their weapons, and forced us to carry their hand grenades. It was a strange position to be in—there I was, stumbling along on the road carrying enough firepower to take out the entire squad of guards, but unable to use it. Even if I managed to throw one or two grenades before being shot, the Germans would retaliate and slaughter all of us. The risk was too great. We had no choice but to put one foot in front of the other.

We marched day and night now. The sound of Allied artillery got louder and louder as they closed in on the last pockets of German resistance.

It became apparent that the Nazis leading us did not know where they were going. Initially, we had set off in an eastern direction, but as the days passed, they had become disoriented, and we had been marching huge circles for some time. Eventually we stopped in a thick forest, unsure how to continue. While the guards argued, the sound of an approaching military motorcycle filled the air, and two high-ranking SS guards soon arrived.

Gesturing with their machine guns, they ordered the group to stand in a line. We all moved to comply, and were soon standing shoulder to shoulder in a clearing in the forest.

'Now,' said one of the SS. 'All Jews, take a step forward.'

Nobody moved. We didn't dare look at each other. The SS were growing impatient and began to yell, when suddenly, all at once, as though we had rehearsed it, everyone took two steps forward. Not just the Jews, but the Dutch, French and Belgian gentiles who marched with us. The SS were furious. Again, they ordered the Jews forward, and again everyone moved forward as one. They did this twice more until the SS finally gave up and rode off. They had orders to murder only the Jews, and did not know what to do in the face of this prisoner solidarity. It was incredibly brave of the non-Jewish men among us. They had risked their lives to save ours.

After that, we walked until we reached a little town called Ostrach. We were marched to the town square, which would usually be used for a market. It was already full of prisoners who had been marched there from camps all across southern Germany. I could see the guards discussing something quietly, and braced for what would come next. I didn't imagine that would be liberation.

I looked away from the guards, and then back again, and in those few seconds they had disappeared—simply vanished. I assume they abandoned their uniforms and tried to disappear into the city as civilians. For the first time in years, we were free.

Moments later we heard the sound of tanks, and an Allied armoured unit rolled into the town square. The army that liberated us were French, although they wore British uniforms, drove American tanks, and carried American weapons and rations. Although we did not have a language in common, they understood our situation, and wanted to help us. They gave us tinned food—not much, just enough that we could eat without getting sick.

While we waited, more people arrived after being liberated from other death marches, some of them in terrible shape. My original group discussed what to do. We welcomed the kindness of the French troops, but we believed that the war could still go in any direction. We'd lived in war-torn Europe long enough to know that, in any given town, the French might be victorious one day, and the Germans the next. So, we decided to find a place to hide and wait for further developments.

We pressed deeper into the village and found a German farmer who was willing to let us sleep in his barn. The barn was very dirty, so in the morning to show our gratitude we cleaned it up as best we could. The next day when the farmer came back from church, he brought with him with a basket of apples for us. Somehow, that basket, the kindness of the farmer, made us truly believe that we were safe. The impossible had finally happened. The war was over for the Germans, and it was over for us. We had survived.

5
After the War

I

W E WERE FREE! WHAT WAS TO BECOME OF US now? We were a group of about a dozen survivors, stranded in the middle of a ruined Germany that was now occupied by Allied troops.

The French army wanted us to help them track down German partisans who had disappeared into the forest to keep fighting their lost cause. We refused. It had been four and a half years since our world had been turned upside down—we'd had enough of war.

Besides, we were mechanics, not soldiers. Our group decided to travel back to the garage in Frommer, which was now run by the French military, to find jobs and start rebuilding our lives.

The journey was about sixty kilometres, and would take us a few days by foot. Although weak, I was in a glorious mood. As I walked, I wandered back and forth over the road, zig-zagging my way down the street purely for the pleasure of not being forced at gunpoint to march in a straight line.

Food was not a problem—whenever we passed a farmhouse, we would knock on the door, explain our situation and ask for help. Nobody turned us away. Civilisation was slowly returning to the land, although reminders of the insanity of the previous years were everywhere. There were piles of rubble where family homesteads had stood for centuries.

For ease of navigation, we walked along the train tracks. At one point on our journey, we found two German train cars abandoned on the tracks. One of them was filled with heavy snow boots with crampons attached—sharp blades used for climbing icy mountains. The other held tailored leather uniforms for French submarine officers. Who can say why? We were a long way from both the alps and the ocean. Naturally, I chose a jacket and trousers for myself, eager to replace the striped uniform from the concentration camp.

We settled in Balingen, close to the garage, where the French Lord Mayor of the city gave me my first identity papers. In order to certify the papers, a photographer took my picture—the first photo taken of me in many years, still wearing the striped concentration camp uniform, our only possession in the world apart from what we had been able to find on our journey home. We also posed for a group photo—the group of Jews who survived by working in the garage. Incredibly, our friend Williams, the very tall fellow who we assumed had been shot on the death march, had survived. He, too, had gone back to Balingen, and joined us for the moment.

On 5 May 1945, in the dying days of World War II, we began to work for the French army, in the same garage we had previously worked for the Germans, using the same tools, but now repairing mainly American vehicles.

On the instruction of the Lord Mayor, I was billeted with a German civilian in her Balingen home. Breakfast came with the room, but the meals were quite small and reflected her poverty. The war had devastated Germany completely, and food for German citizens was in very short supply.

Because I was working for the French, I had access to ration coupons and was able to procure much better food than most of the civilian population at the time. All of a sudden, my standard of living was much better than that of my former persecutors.

Some of the prisoners who had previously been incarcerated at Dautmergen were put in charge of the camp. Meanwhile, the former Nazi guards were now imprisoned in the damp barracks ringed by barbed wire where we'd once been forced to live.

They still lived in relative comfort compared to the conditions we endured, however. When Jews had been imprisoned there, we lived about a hundred people to a barrack. Now, only a fraction of that number were there. Germans were given plenty of space and beds of their own, as well as substantial food rations. Despite this, a friend who was now employed at the camp told me that the former Nazi guards had lodged a formal complaint about having to live in such primitive conditions!

'We can't live like this,' one Nazi had told him. 'This is not fit for a human being.' It was unbelievable to me, the total lack of perspective and empathy from these men who had designed and inflicted far worse conditions on us.

II

The former prisoners of Dautmergen, along with slave labourers from many countries, began to slowly find their way home and look for opportunities to be repatriated to their homelands, which had been freed from fascist occupation. For the most part, the French, Belgian and Dutch prisoners could not wait to go home. The Russians, and

I'm the baby seated to the right, next to my twin sister Bella, visiting our grandmother's house along with our parents and our older brother Joseph. Horodziej, 1922.

Joseph, Bella and I (right) pose for a family portait, Vilna, 1925.

I was always the protective, older (by 20 minutes) brother to Bella. This was taken around 1930.

The crew of the Balingen garage on 5 May 1945, shortly after surviving the Death March, still wearing our prison camp uniforms. I (top row, far left) am pictured with gentle giant Williams (seated centre with crossed arms) and our fast-talking best friend Zis (top row, third from left).

My first ID papers as a free man, provided by the Lord Mayor of Balingen. My ID photo was taken while I was still in my prison camp uniform. The passport photo on the right was taken later, when I felt more human.

Bella and I overjoyed after being reunited in the American zone of occupied Germany, September 1945. When I heard she had survived the Holocaust and learned of her whereabouts, I rode 250 miles on my motorbike to reach her.

With Bella in 1948, shortly before leaving for Australia. Working for the United Nations Relief and Rehabilitation Administration after the war meant I was technically a second-class officer in the French army.

I rarely went anywhere without my camera, as captured in this caricature of me in my French army uniform, including my camera bag, by famous cartoonist Pencula. Balingen, 1948.

The Maisel brothers reunited. Joseph (right) and I in Paris, days before Bella and I embarked for Australia.

My uncle Mischalof poses with me in Sydney on my first day in Australia, January 1949.

With my beautiful bride Miriam Maisel (nee Rohald) on the day of our wedding in Melbourne, 7 September 1956. I had started over and we were happy with our new lives.

Our daughters Yvonne (left) and Michelle build a snowman on a family holiday to Mt Buller in the early 1960s.

Miriam and I at our eldest daughter Michelle's wedding with her husband Leon in 1982.

Proud parents Miriam and I pose with Yvonne and her husband Ron on their wedding day in 1986.

Sixty years later, I'm still the protective older brother. Bella and I are photographed for a State Library of Victoria portrait of Holocaust survivors in 1992.

Receiving a Tattersalls Unsung Hero Award at the Melbourne Jewish Holocaust Centre (JHC) for community service. I'm shaking hands with Shmuel Rosenkranz, director of the JHC, while a Tatterstalls representative applauds, in March 1996.

Miriam and I pose with our grandchildren, Robert, Nathan and Jason, along with fellow grandparent and Michelle's father-in-law, George Deutsch, 1997.

Witnesses to history. JHC AV producer Robbie Simons (right) and I work to digitise a testimony for posterity.

The 2008 Queen's Birthday Honours, with me accepting an Order of Australia Medal for community service from David de Kretser, the 27th Governor of Victoria.

Filming an important commemoration event at the JHC in Melbourne, in 2015.

Bella and I blow out the candles on our 95th birthday in Melbourne, 15 August 2017.

One of my early cameras I used to record the testimonials of survivors. Decades of this work has led to me being called 'the Keeper of Miracles' as I continue my mission to honour the memory of the victims of the Holocaust. To be custodian of their memories and to pass on their stories to the next generation continues to be my responsibility, my privilege, and the greatest miracle of all.

people who came from countries that were now Soviet territories, were less eager. I was reluctant to return to Vilna, which was now occupied by the repressive Soviet Union.

Back in July 1944, Vilna was captured by the Soviet army, and the town was once again swallowed up by the Soviet Union as the capital of the Lithuanian Socialist Soviet Republic. My new identity card classified me as a Polish citizen.

I was a very different man now, and Vilna a different city. The war had changed it forever, and after the Ghetto and the events of the Holocaust it would never be home again. The Jerusalem of Lithuania had been eradicated. Of the more than 200,000 Jews who lived in Lithuania before the war, 95 per cent had been murdered. It was a more complete and devastating annihilation than any other country had suffered at the hands of the Nazis. In Vilna only a few hundred of us survived, mostly partisans who had spent the entire war fighting in the forests around the city.

Now, the Soviet Union was suspicious of those partisans, as well as the non-Jewish intelligentsia who had survived the war. The Soviet authorities informed us that if we returned to the Soviet Union, we would be rewarded and recompensed for our suffering, and sent on holidays. Naturally enough, I was suspicious of this promise. The last time I had been told I was going on holiday I ended up in Stutthof, being beaten and worked to death.

A number of Red Army soldiers were taking the opportunity to flee Soviet countries. One afternoon, two Russian soldiers pulled up outside my garage, each on a 250cc motorcycle. They wanted to trade, so I offered them four litres of petrol in exchange for a bike. Both parties were very happy with the exchange—the Russians climbed onto the one bike and roared off towards the west, and I had my first motorcycle.

Eventually, the garage I was working for was taken over by the United Nations Relief and Rehabilitation Administration (UNRRA), under the supervision of the French Government.

The work was relatively easy, well compensated, and I became good friends with the other mechanics. They were mainly Dutch and Polish people who, like me, did not want to return to the countries that had betrayed them.

Then, abruptly, the French Government cut ties with the UNRRA, so emergency administrators were brought in. The administrators had a great deal of experience dealing with refugees, as they were Russian aristocrats who had fled to France in 1917.

All of a sudden, our supervisors were displaced blue-bloods who spoke a type of very formal French, a peculiar aristocratic dialect that they'd used in the court of Saint Petersburg before the Russian Revolution. They were all unfailingly polite, and it was not a bad development, except that the man they put in charge of my garage knew nothing about cars. It made doing the actual work very difficult, so I began to look for other ways I could be useful.

Fortunately, I was transferred over to UNRRA headquarters, where I took a job as an interviewer, as I spoke several languages shared by the refugee population. It was my job to determine if somebody was a genuine refugee in need of food, clothing and shelter.

Many of the people who applied for refugee status and assistance had not been in concentration camps. Some were collaborators trying to restart their lives after having cooperated with the Germans. Others were opportunists, hoping to make some money by procuring goods and smuggling them across borders, which was much easier to do with the papers provided to refugees.

At the time Germany was divided into four zones: French, American, Russian and British. If one could travel from one zone to another, there was a lot of money to be made by smuggling.

For instance, alcohol was very cheap in the French zone, and American cigarettes were very expensive. Just over the border in the American zone, alcohol was very valuable, and American cigarettes were relatively cheap. As a result, I had to be on the lookout for people falsely claiming asylum in order to pursue smuggling opportunities.

It was here that I first began to practise the skill of interviewing. Those who were being dishonest would tend to slip up and make themselves known during our conversation. A guilty conscience is a terribly heavy thing to carry around.

But so is trauma. I learned that it was important to give people space to speak. If they were genuine refugees, they were mostly in great psychological distress, and often it took them time to work out how to articulate their experiences. Many had lost everything: liberty, livelihood, country, faith and, most importantly, family.

For survivors like them, and like me, being liberated after the war was something of a hollow victory. We had managed to endure everything that had been inflicted on us. It was a type of victory, but it came with the knowledge of how things had been in concentration camps across all of Europe. We had lived through a nightmare and could only imagine how badly our loved ones had suffered. What they had endured and sacrificed to survive. If they had even managed to survive. At this stage, many of those who had survived the concentration camps had no way of knowing if their family had also survived, or where in the world they might be.

III

In my spare time, I began to search for my own family. The postal service had not yet started to function properly, but it was possible for me to have a letter delivered through the French military. I remembered the address of my brother's landlady in Grenoble, and wrote to her asking for any news of Joseph. I got no response.

I was not the only one. Many people were looking for their families after being scattered to camps across Europe. One Sunday in September 1945, a fellow approached me looking for his wife, and asked in Yiddish if there were any Jewish women in this district.

'I'm sorry,' I answered, also in Yiddish. 'There are no Jewish women living here. She must be somewhere else.'

As I spoke, he looked at me strangely. 'You have a very odd Yiddish accent.'

I explained a little about my complicated Lithuanian/ Russian/Polish/Yiddish-speaking family, and told him that my Yiddish was influenced from growing up in Vilna. As I spoke, the man seemed to realise something.

'Look,' he said. 'I've just come from a refugee camp called Lansberg, in the American zone. There's a girl there who speaks with the same accent.'

It was my sister, it had to be.

I set off right away. My supervisor gave me permission

to leave and I jumped on my motorbike, which I rode 250 miles to Bavaria, just outside of Munich, where the Lansberg camp was located.

There she was: Bella. A miracle. We could not believe we had both survived. For some time we just held each other in the middle of the camp, and wept for joy.

I stayed with Bella in Lansberg for two weeks while we searched for my father. I knew where he had been interned at one stage during the war, and that there was a possibility that he might have ended up in one of the many camps for displaced people in the Munich area. From Lansberg, I would ride out and search for clues to my father's fate.

These trips were not without incident. One time, Bella and I were riding on the autostrada, the main highway to Munich. There was hardly any traffic, so I could ride very, very fast. At first I thought we had just been lucky, that we had found the quietest road in all of Germany. Suddenly, an American army jeep appeared on the road, and signalled for me to pull over.

The jeep turned out to be a scout riding ahead of the motorcade of General Eisenhower, the American leader of the occupation forces. They'd cleared the road to ensure he could travel safely to Munich, and somehow I'd slipped past their roadblock and accidentally become an infiltrator behind American lines.

All things considered, General Eisenhower's entourage were very nice. They put my bike on a jeep and offered to escort us to Munich, where we hoped a couple of my father's friends might know where he was. Unfortunately, when we got to Munich, neither of my contacts were home. Bella, the jeep driver and I knocked on the door of first one, and then the other, to no response.

The American driver escorting us said that they could not help any further, and did not know what to do with us, so had no choice but to put us in gaol for the night. In the morning they released us and returned the motorcycle they had confiscated. Unfortunately, they had also confiscated my petrol. The gas tank had been filled with high-octane red petrol supplied by the French army. It was forbidden for civilians to be in possession of it, so they'd siphoned it out of the tank.

I was at a loss, completely stranded in an American army base, until one of the soldiers took pity on me.

'Look,' he said quietly. 'If you go out the gate, you'll find some Germans selling petrol on the black market. We'll look the other way if you have to buy from them.'

So, with the petrol tank full of black-market fuel, we resumed our journey.

I'd never given up hope of finding my father. Whenever I travelled by train, I always walked up and down the station, searching the faces in the crowd for his.

Munich had nearly a dozen displaced person camps nearby, and there was a good chance he had been sent to one of them. Together, Bella and I visited camp after camp, searching for anyone who might know where he was, or have some word of him.

The best clue I had was that I knew he had been imprisoned in Klooga, a particularly remote camp in Estonia, the furthest east towards the Soviet border. It was rumoured that Germany had intended to use it as a base for secret research, and so had placed it as far away from the Allied armies as possible, at a time when they had no fear of the Russians. Its remoteness made it very hard to find information.

Despite all our searching, we could find no trace of my father, until finally I met a man named Merin, who had been in Klooga with him. What Merin told us broke our hearts. My father had not survived the Holocaust. He was able to survive right up until the end of the war, when, with the hope of liberation by the Soviet armies on the horizon, the unimaginable occurred. Just twenty-four hours before the Russians liberated the camp, the Nazis—who had waited too late to evacuate—panicked, and murdered all the Jews in a particularly cruel manner.

The evidence of the killings that the Red Army found remains one of the most chilling reminders of the barbaric reality of the Holocaust. All 2000 Jews imprisoned in

Klooga were ordered to assemble outside, when Merin happened to notice two loose floorboards under his feet. He was able to prise them up and hide under them. He emerged the next day and was the first witness to the murder of all 2000 Jews, including his wife and two children. He was destroyed by what he saw, and asked my sister and me if he could adopt us. He could see no reason to continue living without his family.

Naturally, we said no. We could not replace our father with another who was grieving the loss of his own family. Loss like that cannot be overcome so simply.

I still find it nearly impossible to talk about, even to this day, and for many years I could not stand to think about it. The grief was shattering.

IV

Heartbroken, Bella and I returned to Balingen, where I resumed work.

Two weeks after I was first reunited with Bella, I was back at the garage working underneath a car when I heard a familiar voice calling my name. It was a sergeant in the French army, and he needed me outside right away. I crawled out from under the car and could hardly believe my eyes. It was my brother, Joseph.

Joseph had survived the whole war in France. When it had first broken out, he'd joined the French army and fought on the Italian front. This happened to be the only front where the French were victorious, and after the French surrender, Joseph found himself under the rule of the Vichy puppet government.

His papers identified him as Polish, and so he was able to hide the fact that he was Jewish and escape to a small mining town. He worked as a miner, doing hard physical labour until a farmer named Marcel Vautier offered him shelter. Joseph became part of the Vautier family, and they treated him extremely well.

His former landlady happened to be in contact with him when she received my letter, and let him know that I could be found in Balingen. He'd taken two weeks of leave and set out to find me.

In the space of a couple of weeks I had found my brother and my sister. My life was full. I had feared the worst, but now my siblings and I were reunited.

It was a joyful reunion, but our joy was tempered by the knowledge that we would never see our father again. This remains the great tragedy of my life. I could not forgive myself for the fact that the last time I saw my father we fought bitterly over the merits of communism. I was young, and naive, and because I had read Marx and Engels I thought I knew more about life than him.

The last time I ever saw him was the day of the liquidation of the Ghetto, when he was hiding with Bella in the bunker under our building. When I went out to fight the Estonians, I did not know I would never see him again, or that I would never have the chance to apologise for my stubbornness.

This remains one of my biggest regrets. I know this much—in life you will come to regret the hurt you do to others much more than the hurt that is done to you. More than three-quarters of a century after the Holocaust, the suffering of loved ones haunts me far more than the suffering I personally experienced. This one thing I can never forgive. This is why we must never forget.

6
Starting Over

I

JOSEPH STAYED FOR TWO WEEKS, THEN RETURNED TO France. He was adamant that we accompany him, and although it was tempting, Bella wanted to resume her education and complete her medical degree. So, I remained in Germany to take care of my sister. In time, the headquarters of the UNRRA were moved from Balingen to Ebengen, not far from the famous university town Tübingen. I continued to work there, while Bella took the opportunity to resume studying medicine.

By working for the UNRRA I became a second-class officer in the French army. It was purely an official title; I didn't have to serve in combat, but it meant I wore a French officer's uniform to work, and received all the privileges awarded to French brass.

Less than a year after nearly starving to death in a concentration camp for the crime of being Jewish,

I found myself as a productive, respected member of a society that considered Jewish people human beings and afforded them dignity and respect. An incredible reversal of fortune.

We had a mess hall where we were served good meals, and for one day a month a commissary opened where we were able to buy luxury goods and other items.

Most goods were extremely cheap. My wages were 200 marks, and a bottle of the best champagne was about two marks.

So, in a financial sense, I found myself to be one of the more privileged members of post-war German society. The economy was in ruins, and inflation made cash practically worthless. If you wanted to buy something in a civilian shop, you had to barter. Cigarettes were the most valuable commodity, next to food, perhaps.

I was able to trade half a kilo of coffee for all the textbooks Bella would need to complete her course. Beautiful clothes were freely available on the black market, and for the price of a few meals, traded to once-wealthy Germans who needed bread more than elegant attire, my sister became the best-dressed girl at university.

In 1946 I bought my first camera. The first photos I took were of my Bella. She was a very attractive young woman, extremely photogenic and well-dressed, so I was very pleased with the photos. I would show them to friends and everyone agreed they were wonderful. We also happened to be living in a particularly picturesque part of Germany, so I would hike into the countryside in search of the perfect landscape shots.

My camera and I were inseparable. Ever since that childhood moment in Vilna when the bird alighted on my window, I had wanted to capture the world through a camera—and now I could. The other officers would tease me for carrying it everywhere.

One day, a famous cartoonist, Pencula, visited Ebengen, and was invited to share a meal with us in the officers' mess hall. After the meal, he asked if anyone would like to have a cartoon drawn of them for the price of two packets of cigarettes and I took up the offer. I must say, he captured my likeness very well. I'm standing in my French uniform, with my camera hanging over my back. I still have that cartoon.

In 1948, the UNRRA changed its name to the International Refugee Organization (IRO). Our mission was to repatriate refugees back to their country of origin or, if that was not viable, to a new nation. The destination of choice for most survivors of the Holocaust was the United States of America.

Most European Jews greeted the Americans as liberators, but the ties between European and American Jews went back far longer than World War II. A lot of Jewish people had family in America, people who had emigrated years ago. The cultural influence could be seen in American popular culture; from music to cinema to cuisine. New York in particular was much shaped by the culture of Eastern European Jews. An American charitable organisation even sent the Jewish workers within the IRO a gift of Matzo when Pesach (Passover) approached.

A great many Jewish people were relocating to Israel, following the Zionist promise of the Jewish homeland, and fleeing the Europe that had been home to the Shoah. I considered moving there myself, but a *shlichim*, a Zionist from Israel, visited me and told me that we would not be given first priority to immigrate to Israel as Bella was studying in Tübingen.

Many of my friends who moved to Israel seeking peace found themselves on the frontlines when the Arab–Israeli war broke out in 1948. The Israeli army sent young men with military experience who had no family on the most dangerous missions, on the grounds that they had the least to lose. Survivors of the Holocaust, particularly partisans who had lost their families, made for excellent soldiers.

We stayed in Germany for three and a half years until an opportunity arose for us to leave Europe. It seemed the only sensible option. In Germany, the political situation seemed even more fraught than it had in 1939.

Maria Grodnizka, who was like a mother to Bella, often visited us, and she was no more comfortable in Europe than we were. The reminders that hatred and prejudice did not end with the fall of Hitler were all around us.

In 1947, Maria Grodnizka and I took a bus to visit the Eagle's Nest, the mountaintop house above Hitler's Bavarian summer house, which he used as a diplomatic meeting place. The war was not long over, and the place was still in ruins after being almost obliterated by Allied bombing. The balcony was still intact, so we could stand there and enjoy the same view that Hitler did throughout his rule. We were there, I think, out of morbid curiosity. It was very strange for us to stand in the place where Hitler had dreamt up the nightmares he'd put us through.

Stranger than that, though, were the German tourists all around us. They'd come to pay homage to Hitler, and talked loudly and with great nostalgia about how much they missed him, and how beautiful life had been under his rule.

'He made Germany great again,' one of them said to his friend, not knowing or perhaps not caring that they were standing next to two Holocaust survivors. Extraordinary.

The Soviet Union occupied East Germany, except for West Berlin, where American planes were landing every three minutes to evacuate refugees and to distribute food to a starving population.

The Americans were going out of their way to treat the defeated Germans with respect. The American civilian leadership had learned from the harsh treatment of Germans following World War I. The bitterness caused by the humiliation of defeat, exacerbated by the poverty of the people, had soured into hate and contributed to the rise of Hitler and his brand of populist fascism.

For their part, the military leadership of America expected World War III to break out with the Soviet Union at any minute, and wanted Germany to remain an ally in the conflict they saw as inevitable.

I wanted no part of any war, ever again. I wanted to move as far away as possible, to the other side of the world. Maria made arrangements to move to New York, where she had a relative who was an attorney and could sponsor her immigration. Bella and I had other plans.

My brother had been in touch with my uncle Mischalof, who had moved to Australia and settled in Melbourne years ago. He wrote to me, offering me a chance to start a new life in his adopted country. In a subsequent letter, he included a photo of his family.

They looked like royalty—he was dressed in a beautiful suit with a bow tie, his wife in a sparkling evening gown, two beautiful daughters in formal white dresses. From the photo, I deduced that my uncle must have made himself into a successful and prominent man in this new country.

The photo promised endless opportunity and happiness. After that, I had my heart set on Australia.

II

The first step of the journey would be to travel to Paris. The French army gave me my discharge papers and sent a jeep and driver to escort Bella and me to the border of Germany and France. We travelled light—with the German economy recovering very slowly, there were restrictions on taking money or valuables abroad. I was carrying my new camera—a Leica, a very finely made German camera. It was my prized possession.

A French soldier questioned us before we boarded the train, and he became quite agitated when he found my Leica. He accused me of smuggling it into France to turn a profit, and confiscated it. Luckily I had some photos of myself and Bella, taken with the Leica, so I was able to convince him that I was an amateur photographer, not a professional smuggler. It might not seem important in the scheme of things, but after losing all my photos in the Holocaust, I would have been devastated to lose that camera.

Bella and I arrived in Paris, where we stayed for three weeks near the suburb of Bellevue. Joseph travelled up to visit us for a couple of days. We tried to convince him to come to Australia with us, but was very settled and happy in his new life in a small town close to Avignon. What a feeling to be in Paris! Like many Polish and Lithuanian people of my generation, I idolised French culture. I had dreamed of this city so often I felt I already knew it. The Arc de Triomphe, the Eiffel Tower! For years I had been reading literature from Polish patriots who had escaped to Paris before the war, and I had memorised their loving descriptions of the city so well that I found I knew my way around as though I already lived there. I could take the metro across the city to my destination without consulting a map.

Money was scarce, but I took the advantage of French tailoring to buy myself my first ever adult suit—black and white pinstripe, which was the height of fashion at the time. My sister didn't buy anything, as she already had a very fine wardrobe, and every franc was precious.

We wanted very much to experience the theatre in Paris. Tickets to the Tivoli were fifty francs, nearly all the money had, but we decided it was worth it. We entered, but the usherette refused to allow us to take our seats. I was confused at first, then began to feel uneasy, and then angry. Was this anti-Semitism? Were we being refused service because we were Jewish?

Eventually the usher took us aside and quietly explained that the ushers made no money, and relied on tips to survive. We'd spent every franc we had on the tickets, so had nothing to tip her. I explained this, and eventually she relented, and grumpily allowed us to take our seats.

It was a valuable lesson: the French will not be shy about refusing you service if they feel they have a justifiable grievance. We learned this lesson again when, after a very pleasant stay in Paris, we travelled to the port of Marseille, where our ship to Australia had been grounded by a maritime strike.

It was more than a month before we could find alternate passage on a French military vessel called the *Eridan*. The boat was travelling to Sydney, via several of the former French colonies in the Pacific, where they would drop off battalions of French troops and pick up the old garrison to take them home. We could accompany the troops to the Pacific, and then on to Australia. Together, Bella and I waved goodbye to Europe, and watched the ruined continent disappear over the horizon.

7

She'll Be Right

I

THE VOYAGE LASTED TWO MONTHS. THE FOOD WAS terrible, but there was plenty of French wine, all you could drink. This helped pass the time, although most of us could not drink very much. The ship was relatively small, and was thrown this way and that by the waves, so many of us were seasick. It was not a proper passenger vessel, but the cargo hold had been fitted out with mattresses, which were not at all steady in rough seas and quite foul-smelling after a few days. Whenever possible Bella and I tried to sleep on deck, in the fresh air.

We stopped in Tahiti, where the custom was for locals to come out and greet the arrival of a ship with ceremonial welcome and ball. The young women of the village came out to dance with us, and I struck up a conversation with one who spoke immaculate French. She had been the star pupil of her Tahitian school, and after graduation had been rewarded with a trip to Paris.

'I love Paris,' I told her. 'What did you think?'

'I hated it,' the girl said. She'd spent her entire time in Paris feeling homesick and dreaming of coming back to Tahiti to sit on a clifftop and watch the sun set over the sea. The conversation was something of a revelation for me. For my whole life I had viewed Paris as the centre of the civilised world, and this was my first brush with a culture with a completely unique set of cultural norms and priorities. All through the evening I was struck by the realisation that the world was so much wider and grander than I'd ever imagined. It was a wonderful feeling.

I spent the rest of the voyage trying to improve my English, of which I had taken two years in school, and understood the basics, but knew would be important in our new lives. I worked very hard to improve my fluency, only to finally reach Australia and discover that the language they spoke was nothing like the formal, British English I'd been taught.

'G'day,' people would say to me, or, 'She'll be right, mate'. What on Earth could that mean? Who is 'she'? Why wouldn't she be alright?

When we finally reached Sydney, in January 1949, the waters were not deep enough for our ship to berth at Circular Quay, so we were put into smaller boats to make landfall.

We European immigrants were baffled by the sky-scrapers we saw shining in the city. A rumour spread that we had boarded the wrong ship and had secretly been brought to New York. Our vision of Australia was one of beaches, and flat land. The only thing I knew about it was that Australians liked to drink a great deal of beer, and that there were more sheep than people.

Our uncle was already expecting us, and had hired a little boat to come out and meet us. I still have a photo I snapped of him waving to us from the water.

We stayed a few days in Sydney, and the first thing we did was visit an Australian restaurant. My uncle ordered for us, and it was the first time I experienced Australian-style sandwiches, made with fresh white bread sliced very thin. I ate five in a row before my uncle stopped me. He didn't understand what the journey over had been like, and that we were still half-starved.

The train to Melbourne was another revelation. To travel by train in Europe means to pass a constantly changing vista: towns, farms, forests. Australia seemed to be nothing but endless, empty space. It made no sense to my brain that the cities would be so far apart, and so sparsely populated. When we reached the state border, the gauge of the railway changed, so the train had to be lifted and placed on the new tracks. It was surprising—not something you see every day!

Then we arrived at Spencer Street station, which was another surprise, this one a little unpleasant. I was appalled. In Europe, the railway station was usually one of the most prestigious buildings in the city. It was a point of pride for travellers to arrive in Paris, Berlin or Vienna and be greeted by marble floors and vast halls. Here, instead of grandeur, there were concrete platforms and an iron shack. I began to wonder if I'd made a mistake coming to this country that couldn't even afford a proper railway station.

My uncle ordered a taxi to take us from Spencer Street to his house in Carlton. We travelled down Royal Parade, and I thought that surely none of the buildings on either side of me were good enough for my uncle. Eventually we turned into a narrow street in Carlton, and the taxi stopped. We could see a little terrace house, barely six metres across. I originally thought that the taxi driver had made a mistake, or was stopping for lunch, and my heart sank when I realised this was where my uncle lived.

As I would learn, my uncle was not a rich man—the photo of him wearing an expensive suit had been taken at a wedding—but he did have a heart of gold.

My extended family in Australia went to great lengths to make me feel at home. I had a cousin, Mordi Slonim, who got me at job at Preston Motors, a Clifton Hill garage. I arrived in Melbourne on a Thursday and interviewed for the job on the following Monday.

The interview was very brief. The foreman of the garage invited me into his office, where he asked me if I spoke English. I nodded.

'What's this then?' He pointed at the phone on his desk.

'Telephone,' I said.

'Pick it up and say something.'

I reached over and picked up the receiver. 'Hello?'

The foreman nodded again. 'Good enough.'

II

My job was as a cleaner. I had to sweep the garage and lubricate the cars. Strangely enough, it was a very similar job to my first task at that garage in Vilna all those years ago. On my first day, while sweeping, I found three pennies on the floor. I assumed that somebody in the garage had dropped their money and would be back for it eventually, so I left them where they had fallen, and swept carefully around them.

After a few days I was called into the office and told off. The boss wanted to know why I wasn't sweeping properly. I tried to explain my reasoning regarding the pennies, but he didn't listen. The way he spoke to me was very disrespectful, and it left a bad taste in my mouth.

The same day, G.J. Coles, the wealthy businessman who owned the supermarket chain, brought his Rolls-Royce in to be serviced. When I finished the job, he approached me and thanked me for my work. I spoke almost no English, so struggled to understand him, which didn't bother him in the slightest. He handed me two shillings—a decent amount of money at the time—and shook my hand. This unnerved me almost as much as the boss yelling at me. I was used to the class distinctions of old Europe. Here, a man who drives a Rolls-Royce shakes the hand of his mechanic? It would take me a while to get used to the way things were done in this country.

I was told to change the tyres on a car. Unbeknownst to me, in Australia, this was a straightforward job—you undid four nuts, removed the entire wheel, and replaced it with another, identical part. The whole thing takes a moment. In Germany, if someone asked me to 'change the tyres', it would mean taking the actual rubber tyre off the wheel hub and replacing it with new rubber. So this is what I did, a complicated and difficult procedure.

I was three hours into the task when the foreman came by.

'What are you doing?' He was exasperated. 'What's the matter with you?'

I tried to explain to him that I was following the instruction I had been given, but it only made him angrier. It was very demoralising, to be treated so disrespectfully by the foreman when I was doing my best to follow his orders. The insult was made worse by the fact that I was an extremely capable auto-electrician and mechanic, and used to being treated with some level of respect.

I walked off the job. It was true that I needed the money, but not as much as I valued my dignity. My new job only lasted a week, which wasn't even long enough to collect one pay cheque. Luckily for me, the office girl ran after me and insisted I take the money for the days I'd worked. She even counted in some overtime I hadn't known I'd done, paying me much more money than I had expected to earn. I almost walked back in. My dignity was valuable, but was it *that* valuable?

In the end, I went home and told my cousin I couldn't work there anymore. The garage was neglected, the equipment wasn't clean; it just didn't live up to the standards I was used to.

He took me to a dealership in the city called Keller Faulkner, on Russell Street, which was selling high-end automobiles like Rolls-Royces and Bentleys. They checked my English again, which was already improving. This time they also tested my mechanical knowledge, and I passed with flying colours.

The foreman there was a very nice chap. He never yelled, and he took the time to patiently explain anything I did not immediately understand due to the language barrier.

One time he even told me off for working too fast. A customer had dropped his car off with a broken radio. I opened it up, found a faulty fuse and replaced it, repairing the radio in five minutes. The foreman took me aside and gave me a little talk.

'Look,' he said. 'The firm can't send the customer a bill for five minutes work. We need to charge him for at least an hour, or the boss will be unhappy. So find a way to take a whole hour on this job.' He explained that he didn't want anyone in his shop working too fast, because the longer it took to get the job done, the more workers would be needed, which meant he would be able to justify a large staff during union negotiations. So I went back and listened to the radio for an hour just to make sure that it worked perfectly. The next day the customer picked up the car and was very pleased with the way it sounded— and the firm was happy with the price we charged.

My next task was to repair a starter motor, a job that should have taken an hour. In the process, I lost one of the screws necessary to repair it and couldn't find it. I was reluctant to go to the store to buy a replacement, as my English wasn't good enough to ask for precisely what I needed. Instead, I spent a stressful half-hour looking for the screw, finally finding it. When the foreman came by to check on me, I was still working on the starter motor. He was delighted.

'Everyone, come here and look at Phillip,' he told them. 'This is how I want all of you to be working. There's no need to rush.'

Australia was not how I expected it to be at all.

III

Slowly, I began to adjust to life in this new country. There was already a Jewish community established in Melbourne—mostly of Anglo-Saxon descent. Perhaps it was rather embarrassing for them, having assimilated into mainstream Australian society, only to be assailed by a wave of Eastern European cousins with completely different habits and diets, some with strict religious beliefs, all talking with their hands and yelling in broken English. They called us the 'Greeners', as in 'green wood' or 'people who are not yet mature'.

I must say, Australia was very good to us. In Yiddish, we 'Greeners' called it *Di Goldene Medinah*, 'The Golden Country'. People were extremely welcoming, Jews and Gentiles alike.

For my first year or so in Australia, my English was not the best. Sometimes I would become stuck while trying to express myself, and the Australian I was talking to would just pat me on the shoulder and say, 'You're okay, mate. Take your time. She'll be right.' In this way, I grew to understand what that phrase meant, and to deeply appreciate the philosophy behind it. No one understands better than a refugee how precious the egalitarian nature of Australian society is. Here, everyone treated me as a human being—they took it for granted that everyone should be treated with respect.

Bella, who was always the more extroverted of the two of us, adjusted to life in Australia very well. She worked in my cousin Mordi Slonim's dress factory, and after six months met and fell in love with a businessman named Markus Hirshorn, originally from Białystok but now well established in Australia. They had a whirlwind romance and were married.

In 1956, seven years after arriving in my new country, I married an Australian woman, Miriam Rohald. She was Jewish, but born in Australia, and she was a typical Australian in every way—relaxed, very easygoing, taking life as it came.

In contrast, I was a typical Holocaust survivor: always tense, constantly rushing round trying to make the most of every minute. We were opposite personalities really, but sometimes that makes for the best marriage.

Miriam was a very good dancer. She was also an

exceptional pianist. She'd passed the teachers' exam at the London Music Academy and was a certified music instructor, although she never worked as one. When we met, she was working in a big warehouse in Spencer Street as an office girl.

Miriam was from a good home. Her father, prior to emigrating to Australia, held the prestigious position of being the secretary to the famous Chief Rabbi of Palestine—Rabbi Cook. His name was Naftali, and he was a very quiet, serious and scholarly fellow. When he was at a party and someone was trying to make small talk about a topic that did not interest him, he would move his chair to the corner of the room, pull out a book and start reading. By contrast, Miriam's mother was extremely practical. She ran a tight ship and insisted that everything be done properly and to schedule.

Every so often on a Friday, I would take my mother-in-law into the city and wait in the car while she went about her business. At the time, I'd invested in some shares, which had immediately plunged in value. One afternoon, while escorting my mother-in-law to town, I bought a paper and saw that the shares had gone up to the level I'd originally bought them at. I wanted to rush to a phone to sell them, but my mother-in-law forbade it.

'It's Friday,' she said. 'We have to get home right away to start cooking the meal. Do it next week.'

I did not argue, and took her straight home. By Monday, the shares had doubled in price, and I sold them for a tidy profit.

Life is unpredictable, but in those years I was very lucky, especially when it came to my wife. We were very happy.

Miriam and I bought a little house, one half of a split duplex in South Caulfield, and about a year later Miriam became pregnant with our first child.

At nine months, very soon before the baby was due, we were driving home from the cinema one evening when a car sideswiped us. It was a very serious accident, and both cars were destroyed, although luckily neither of us suffered more than a scratch.

I was distraught. When we got home, I was naturally very upset, but Miriam just sat down and invited me calmly to sit with her.

'Let's have a cup of tea,' she said, 'and we can discuss the matter.'

And that was my life with Miriam. She took things in her stride; it took a great deal to upset her. She calmed me down and assured me that the child would be fine. Sure enough, before long, our first daughter, Michelle, was born.

I was not at all relaxed about it. I could not believe how beautiful the baby was. It seemed to me an absolute historical certainty that this was the cutest baby that had ever been born. I took a photo of her and printed off about fifty copies, then sent friends and family a few copies each. One for them, and some spares just in case they wanted to distribute them to colleagues.

About eighteen months later, we had our second beautiful daughter, Yvonne. These were the best years. To have children is the greatest joy a person can experience in life, and this fact is not lost on any survivor of the Holocaust. Hitler, and the hatred he inspired, tried to murder me and everyone like me. He failed, and when I brought a child into the world, it was the only sensible countermeasure to that kind of hatred. Love.

To hold my daughters in my arms the day they were born. To walk them to school on their first day, to walk them down the aisle on their wedding day. These moments are wonderful in the life of any parent, but imagine how precious they are to us survivors. When we were starving, freezing, and being tortured for no reason beyond hatred and prejudice, who could have imagined that life could be so good?

My daughters and wife taught me to be more like them—peaceful and satisfied with life. Miriam was a good influence on me. She made the most of every day, would go to the movies, read her romantic books, calm me down whenever I was stressed.

One time, she shook me awake in the middle of the night and told me she needed to tell me something: 'Phillip, I don't want to upset you, but I have some bad news.'

'You don't want to upset me!' I cried out, immediately upset. 'What is it?'

'Well, don't be upset,' she said in a gentle voice, 'but the house is on fire.'

Luckily when I jumped out of bed to find the source of the smoke we could smell, it was only some rubbish burning in the incinerator at the back of the house.

Miriam was a very good partner in life. I was working extremely hard, days and nights, trying to be a good provider and to secure our future financially, and was very careful with money.

Every spare penny went straight into the bank, and eventually the bank manager called me in and asked me what I planned to do with my money.

'What do you mean?' I was baffled by his question. 'These are my savings.'

'But aren't you interested in investing?' he asked. 'Why aren't you making interest off this capital?'

I stared at him. This hadn't crossed my mind. I had spent my formative years as a devoted socialist. Capitalism took some getting used to. In the end, I asked him what he thought would make a good investment, and he advised me to buy a taxi licence.

I thought it over, and it seemed like a good plan, so I leased a small workshop at the Black and White Cabs taxi depot and bought a taxi. Now I worked in the garage during the day and had to drive my taxi at night. In time, I saved up enough for another taxi, so I bought two and hired a driver, then another. Eventually, I was able to buy and manage a fleet of six taxis.

I worked very long hours. My family were wonderful about it. On some occasions Miriam would stay up late at night, waiting for me to come home from repairing a car that had broken down in the middle of the night. My daughters would write me letters telling me about their day because I could not always be there.

Eventually we accumulated some money and invested in an apartment block in St Kilda. It was a good price, and a fine investment, but we couldn't find a manager to look after the apartments and tenants for us, so we decided to move in for a few months until we could find someone. Those few months turned into eleven years.

IV

As you can imagine, these were very strenuous years. While I was working day and night, Miriam had to manage the apartment block. For years we were not able to go away together on a family holiday. Someone always had to stay home to look after things.

It was a fairly basic apartment block, lacking luxuries such as hot water, and with all residents sharing the communal toilet. It did have a large backyard, in which I installed a carport where I could repair taxis, and friends' cars.

Our tenants came from all over the place and from all walks of life. They rented individual rooms, and there was a shared kitchen that catered to everyone.

The kitchen was the site of a daily row between two women, one Catholic and one Protestant. Every night they would insist on cooking their meal on the same part of the stove, at the same time, and would bicker about it. This went on for years, until finally the Catholic woman got fed up and left. The Protestant woman was triumphant for a day, cooked her meals in peace for a week, and then packed her own things and left. She did not know how to fill her days without her enemy, and ended up missing her like a loved one.

With the cosmopolitan make-up of the tenants, the

apartment block was a wonderful little community. Some of them became as close to us as family. If somebody in the apartment was ill, Miriam would cook them meals, sometimes for months at a time, and the tenants grew loyal to us.

There was one woman, visiting from Queensland, who loved living there so much that she asked us to keep her room for her while she went back to Queensland to settle her affairs. We agreed, and then didn't see her for two years. Then, one day, she turned up at the door with her suitcase and paid for the room in full.

Another fellow we grew close to was Terry. Terry was a habitual drunk. He was nice man, totally harmless, but a severe alcoholic. He'd moved in and initially managed to keep himself more or less together. He found himself a girlfriend, and life was going well for him. Then he found out his girlfriend had been unfaithful, and he started to drink. For three weeks he drank without a break, at which point I decided he needed help. I took him to a rehabilitation facility for alcoholics on Victoria Parade. The woman in charge, a stern Jewish woman, tested his blood alcohol levels and sent him away because he was not drunk enough.

So, he went home and kept right on drinking for another three weeks. This time he was more than drunk enough to be accepted for rehabilitation.

I picked him up after a few weeks. On the drive home, Terry turned to me.

'Do you know what that bloody woman said to me?' he asked. 'She said, "Terry, you'll never learn your lesson. You're going to be a drunk your whole life. You'll be back here in no time."'

'What did you say?' I asked.

'I said I'd show her,' said Terry. 'Nobody is going to tell me what to do.' And just like that, Terry stopped drinking. He never touched a drop again.

At 5 pm every day, at shift change, my taxi drivers would bring the cars around and I would fix them in the backyard.

The taxi drivers were a funny mob. One night, one of my drivers broke down in the middle of the city and called me to come and repair the car. I found the problem quickly enough. The driver had been driving with the handbrake on his whole shift, continuously pressing the clutch in order the get the car to move. He'd burned it out completely.

'What are you doing driving around with the handbrake up!' I exclaimed. 'You've ruined the clutch!'

'It's not my fault!' the driver yelled back. 'The guy driving the car before me put it on!'

Unbelievable. Even more unbelievable, I couldn't find anyone to replace him, so I couldn't sack him.

V

Life was busy, but the Holocaust lingered over everything, like a shadow over my life. I never discussed it with Miriam. We could never find a way to talk about it—the difference in experience was too vast. Back then, those who had survived the Holocaust never discussed it with those who hadn't experienced it. There was no way they would understand.

Whenever the Holocaust was represented in the media, I sought it out. I would read every book I could get my hands on, and watch every film that was broadcast, but when I turned them on, my wife would leave the room. When we had her friends over, we would discuss current events: the news, sports, pop culture, gossip and social occasions. When we saw my friends, fellow survivors, we only ever discussed the Holocaust. We could speak of nothing else. There had to be some outlet for all that trauma.

In the fifties and sixties, if we tried to explain what had happened, nobody believed us. Who could believe that an entire nation could be so systematically cruel?

That a whole society could stand by while such atrocities occurred? From the comfortable, peaceful suburbs of Australia, it didn't seem possible.

Even my own uncle didn't believe me. When he asked me how I survived, I tried to relay the events in a very mild, sanitised retelling, as I did not want to upset him. He thought I was crazy, that I was making up wild fantasies. My own uncle! I gave up trying to make him understand.

Like many survivors, I wanted to protect my children from the trauma of the Holocaust, so I only told them fragments of my past.

VI

The years passed, and our daughters grew up and made us very proud. We were blessed to attend their university graduations, and then their weddings.

Michelle married first, to a young gentleman named Leon Deutsch, then Yvonne married Ron Sherwin. Both had very big, very lovely weddings.

After Miriam and I came home from Yvonne's wedding, we stood in the living room and started to cry. The house was empty. What would we do with our lives now?

We decided that once a year we would take a month off work, and would travel the world. We travelled far and wide, saw the whole world. I carried a video camera with me everywhere I went, and Miriam carried a backup still camera for me. She was the greatest wife I could ever have asked for, but also learned to be a very capable photographer's assistant!

We travelled to Europe, Israel, the United States, all through China—which was undergoing rapid transformation after the cultural revolution—and to Russia when it was still under the thrall of communism. They were wonderful experiences.

As the years passed, our daughters provided us with many happy occasions, none more so than when our three grandsons were born—Robert, Jason and Nathan. It was an immense privilege to celebrate their bar mitzvahs and be present at their university graduation ceremonies.

Each of them has been to Israel, and Robert and Nathan participated in the March of The Living, an international program to pay respect to the victims of the Holocaust. Jason was a member of the Australian junior cricket team for the Maccabiah Games, where he won a bronze medal.

I am so proud of the fine young men they have become. As well as being extraordinary individuals, they are also a symbol of the victory over Hitler's plan to annihilate the Jewish people.

Bella had two children, Michael and Janice, who would go on to achieve great success in their lives, and provide her with two grandchildren, and four great-grandchildren.

Back in Europe, Joseph lived a happy life in his small French village. We wrote often, but no matter how hard Bella and I lobbied him to come and live with us he could not be convinced to leave France. Then in 1963 I got a telegram from Joseph letting me know he was very ill with late-stage cancer, and had been hospitalised in Avignon. I dropped everything I was doing and raced over to him. It took me some time to track him down, going from hospital to hospital until I finally located him. He was very weak, but recovered slightly, and we had another five months with him.

Later in the sixties, Miriam fell ill with a goitre. It was very, very serious. She suffered from a very high temperature and they took her to the Alfred Hospital to give her radiation treatment. She stayed there for a few weeks and suffered terribly from the treatment. This was the first time since the Holocaust that I felt so helpless.

She recovered, thankfully, but from then on, she developed a suspicion of doctors, and refused to see them. The only doctor she trusted was a friend, who looked after her for the rest of her life.

We were married for forty-seven years, a wonderfully happy time. After she passed on from this world, in 2003, I would never be the same, but I treasure every moment we had, and try to live every day as she would have. Time is always shorter than we think, and I try to make the most of life.

I do not believe in living a life in opposition to the Holocaust, in letting those who oppressed and tormented me dictate the terms of my life. But if I did, well, I'd like to think that I have won. My children prosper, my culture flourishes, photos of my grandchildren smile at me from my wall. They are alive, and embrace the world, and they are happy.

8

The Keeper of Miracles

I

A S THE YEARS PASSED, SOME SURVIVORS COULD
not find peace. No matter our circumstances, most
of us felt the need to mark what had happened in
an official sense. This need grew more urgent as time went
on, and led our community in Melbourne to establish a
permanent museum, one of the first in the world.

The Jewish Holocaust Centre (JHC) was the culmina-
tion of many years of hard work, by many people, notably
members of Kadimah—the Jewish Cultural Centre—and
the Bund—the Jewish socialist organisation—along with
many more who were instrumental in establishing it.
We are particularly grateful to Abe Goldberg, one of our
strongest contributors over many years.

The official opening was in March 1984, an auspicious
day not only for survivors, but also our families and our
wider community. Hundreds of people gathered in the car

park of 13 Selwyn Street, Elsternwick for the ceremony. It was one of those Melbourne days that promises rain and then surprises you with tremendously hot weather, and the crowd sheltered from the sun under their official programs. Several prominent members of the community gave speeches.

The JHC was one of the first dedicated Holocaust museums founded anywhere in the world outside the sites of the atrocities. This was largely due to the sheer number of survivors who found refuge in Melbourne. In the decade after the Holocaust, the Jewish population of Australia doubled. This was especially visible in Melbourne, where over half the survivors settled—particularly Polish-speaking people. A survivor in our community once joked that older people in Melbourne generally come from 'English stock, Irish stock, or Białystock'.

The JHC was driven by one guiding principle: that survivors were our greatest resource. They were our guides, people who could serve as authentic witnesses to history and share their stories. There is no greater way to help someone truly understand your story than to share it in person. The JHC was to be a living museum, with survivors of historical events able to recount those events.

Every year, tens of thousands of school students from city and country Victoria visit the centre and are educated about the events of the Holocaust. For many, this might be the first time they have met a Jewish person. They learn about humanity and the importance of standing up against hatred and bigotry. This was our mission from day one, and it remains so.

My own involvement in the JHC began very humbly, when a woman named Ursula Flicker asked for my assistance. I had met Ursula in 1982, when members of our community were arranging artefacts for an exhibition to commemorate the Holocaust. Ursula asked me to write a remembrance on the destruction of the Vilna Ghetto.

Two years later, when the JHC was established, Ursula volunteered as the centre's archivist, and would spend over twenty years collecting, supervising and documenting artefacts of the Holocaust.

Ursula was from Białystock, a Polish city that had an extremely close-knit Jewish community. Even after the Holocaust, people from Białystock reunited and formed a society to keep the community alive.

Ursula survived the Holocaust because of a great tragedy. The SS came to her house when she was seventeen. They needed to fulfil their quota of Jews to transport to the camps. Of course, they did not say this to young Ursula. Rather, they lied and told her they needed a volunteer to go to a convalescent home—basically, on a holiday. She wanted to give her younger sister, the opportunity for an easier life, so she sent her sister in her place.

Naturally, her sister was taken to a concentration camp, where she perished. Ursula escaped into Siberia and survived the war in Russian territory, but her actions would torment her for the rest of her days.

The feeling of guilt was with her each morning when she woke up, and each night when she went to bed. It became an obsession, and the driving force behind her work.

Most of us who have worked in the JHC have something like this that drives us. For me, it is the promise I made to my friends in that camp in Estonia, to tell the world what had happened. Naturally, when Ursula asked for my assistance, I said yes. At first, I offered a donation, but she wanted something else.

'Thank you,' she said. 'But anyone can give money. Not everyone can do the kind of work we need. There is another way you can help us.'

II

Ursula needed a photographer to help catalogue the collections. I worked for two years in the archives, carefully photographing documents and photos from the Holocaust that could be used for exhibitions and educational purposes.

One day, the JHC procured an artefact that broke my

heart. It was called 'The Album'—a book of photographs by SS photographers at Auschwitz, and a record that chronicled the daily life of prisoners. It showed how they arrived, how they were segregated and where they were processed before being taken to the gas chambers and crematorium.

The images in that book shook me to my core. I don't think I had a proper night's sleep for three weeks after I put it down. The faces in the photos haunted me. I was struck by the little details—the coat one man wore to keep him warm as he walked to his death. These were real people, individuals with stories that started before the Holocaust, and tragically, for the most part, ended there. Who were these people? Who remembered them now, so many years later? The lost lives, and the stories behind them, began to haunt me. More than six million Jews died during the Holocaust. Six million. How can a person make sense of that? The enormity of the crime is unimaginable. Try and hold in your mind what six million people might look like. Even one million. One million of anything at all.

What does a million grains of sand look like? A million flakes of snow? A million dead people? Our minds cannot conceive of such numbers, let alone the scale of the atrocity. A young person, born in safety in Australia, on the other side of the world from Nazi Germany, will find little to identify with in this number.

However, it is possible to identify with one person, with one individual story. There is common ground to be discovered. When one human being entrusts another with their story, empathy can develop—across generations, and across the years. Particular details from a story will jump out and remind somebody of their own life. Suddenly, they can understand.

What is it about a personal story that makes it so powerful? There is some human element that allows us to understand another person's experience, even if that experience is far beyond our frame of reference, because every human being has common needs and fears. Deep down, the things that make us tick are all the same.

I became determined to do more to record the personal experiences of survivors. It was an enormous task.

The JHC already had an oral history project in place. Since the 1980s, a team of volunteers led by Sandra Cowan and Jenny Wajsenberg, and later Anne Bernhaut, had conducted over 200 audio and video recordings. It was initially run on an ad-hoc basis, and was rarely a priority.

Anne was a pharmacist with a business to run, so could dedicate only limited time to the project, which at the time was recording around thirty testimonials a year. Ten months might go by without a new one being made. I volunteered to begin organising more regular testimonials. With the passing years, I began to feel a great sense of urgency, anxious to capture every story possible.

By this time, I was seventy. People of my generation were passing away more and more frequently, so I wanted to make interviewing survivors and recording their testimonies a priority.

As I was retired, I was available to work on the project full-time, so gradually, at the suggestion of the JHC, I took over recording the testimonials.

III

The first testimonial I recorded on video was in 1992. Prior to the interview, I went to the survivor's home and we created a questionnaire that would be the template for interviewing her and other survivors into the future.

The testimonial ran to four hours in total, and we were both exhausted by the end of it. Even so, I wanted to record another immediately. It seemed to me there was no time to waste, and I began to actively seek out survivors to speak to.

We began to record interviews more frequently. I would want to record at least five days a week, and at times we had interviews scheduled six days a week. We took a break on Saturdays, but recorded on Sundays so those who worked full-time still had an opportunity to participate.

For me, it was more than a full-time role. The project took over my life in many ways. It took priority over nearly everything else. There were many days my daughter Yvonne would visit me at work to deliver the lunch I had forgotten in my rush to get back to the JHC.

At first, we focused on collecting testimonies of the Holocaust, describing what had happened to the person. But we soon realised that we had another infinitely valuable resource available. These people were the last members of Jewish communities from all over Europe; communities that had been completely destroyed. They could provide us with information that existed nowhere else on Earth—about *shtetls*, lives and communities that had been wiped out, the names of Jewish families that had been completely annihilated. Each survivor was a living tribute to all that we had lost. The small details of the past—there is no replacement for them when they pass unrecorded from memory.

Convincing people to share their stories was not always easy. Some of these people had not wanted to talk about the Holocaust for forty years. It was too difficult.

Survivors record testimonials for different reasons. For some, it is cathartic; others feel a sense of obligation towards those who died. Some simply want to document and validate the experience of the Holocaust, for those who want detailed knowledge, and for those who simply cannot believe what had happened.

I was present at every interview we did. I served as moral support, and helped survivors keep track of dates and places.

All our interviewers were volunteers, and most were tremendously busy. We had professionals who could only volunteer one day of the week. People still had to make a living, after all.

It is important to note that the JHC was a labour of love. It was run entirely by volunteers, and everyone who volunteered donated their money as well as their time. Resources were very scarce—I would have to bring in my own pencils and erasers, and I would use my own computer to do our printing.

We didn't have any money to build a proper studio, so we improvised. The JHC gave us the use of a little shed at the back of the museum and our volunteers did the rest. The roof was leaking, so we installed an artificial flower where the water dripped down, and joked to visitors that it was an irrigation system to help the flower grow.

We found some old insulation panels and installed

them through the shed at the back of the JHC, then draped lengths of black cloth to create a backdrop to film against.

The shed was a very narrow room, only a couple of metres across and about the length of two dining tables, but it was a cosy, intimate space. Something about the close quarters helped people to feel comfortable, and to forget where they were, allowing them to completely submerge themselves in their memories.

Years later, when we transferred to a bigger room and better facilities, I found myself missing the shed we started in. I missed the intimacy of our first, ramshackle studio. The new one was wonderfully appointed, completely soundproofed, but it lacked the feeling of being some kind of sacred space.

There was a large parking space on Orrong Road where people would dump their rubbish, from which we scavenged materials—shelves, cabinets and other useful items for the centre. Without the selfless contribution of dozens of people over the years, it would have been impossible to achieve what we did. Those who conducted the interviews were especially valuable. A good interviewer is rare, but over the years we built a wonderful team.

One of our first and most distinguished volunteers was a fellow called Gerhardt Brunotte. During the Holocaust, his father had been a very important German official stationed in a town in Silesia. When Gerhardt was about eight years old, he saw a group of Jews being taken away for transport to the concentration camps. He didn't really understand what he was seeing, but he saw a little girl, not much older than him, who was carrying a doll. She dropped the doll, and an SS guard noticed and walked over to her. Instead of helping, he kicked the doll down the road, and then kicked the little girl, sending her sprawling into the mud.

Gerhardt never forgot this incident. When he grew up, he immigrated to Australia, and years later, haunted by the memory of this girl, became one of our dedicated volunteers.

Gerhardt was instrumental in establishing the Testimonials Project. He would help whenever he could, in any way he could imagine. One day it occurred to him that the project should have its own symbol, so he designed a logo to use on all our stationery and correspondence.

We also had an outstanding interviewer named Geri Kras. Before each interview she took care to establish a good relationship with the interviewee, sharing little details of her own life to build rapport.

People can be very gifted but still not make ideal interviewers. For example, once we had a volunteer who was a very skilled lawyer, but he couldn't stop himself from interrogating the poor survivors.

'Can I just clarify what you've just told me?' he would say after hearing a particularly horrifying story, 'because on a previous occasion you behaved in a markedly different way to the manner you're describing now. I'm just trying to get it all down for the record.' He meant well, but his style was perhaps not ideal for the work we were undertaking.

The skills that make a good interviewer are highly specific. Everyone took a different approach, but the best ones all had certain traits and skills in common. One had to know the history of the Holocaust back to front. Most of our interviewers spoke more than one language—for survivors and witnesses from the first generation, we were taking testimonials in five languages.

Occasionally, I would conduct the interview myself. It was necessary, because sometimes a survivor really needed to give their testimonial to someone who spoke the same language.

Being able to deliver their testimony in their preferred language makes a huge difference to a survivor who has not previously spoken about the trauma of their past. When speaking in their mother tongue, people are able to express themselves with an eloquence and accuracy that can otherwise escape them, even if they have mastered English over the years.

IV

When I say 'the same language', I don't just mean that we both spoke Yiddish or Polish. I mean we shared a frame of reference, one that only other survivors can understand.

If I were to tell you, 'I was hungry', most people would relate this to having missed breakfast, or being too busy to eat lunch. The word 'hunger' means something very different to Holocaust survivors. It means not eating for three or four days at a time, until you grow so weak the emptiness in your stomach becomes the centre of your world.

To us, the word 'selection' does not mean having to make a choice. Rather, it means having no choice at all, having your life stripped away from you. It brings to mind people standing naked in the freezing cold while an SS officer decides if they will be taken away and killed that day, or if it will be their best friend standing next to them instead.

It is hard for us even to hear the word 'gas' when talking about appliances or heating without bringing the gas chambers to mind. No, we speak our own language, that of a shared experience, one that is unimaginable to anyone who did not live it.

There is such a wide variety of stories of survival. There are people who suffered mentally and physically and endured the hardships of the concentration camps. Jews who lived as Christians on false papers, looking over their shoulders every moment. Then there are those who escaped into the forest and lived out the war as partisans, taking revenge against the Nazis. And there are those who survived through collaboration—stories of heroism and cowardice and everything in between. Naturally people make movies, and write books, but then, of course, poetic licence creeps in. It is very hard to tell a story without injecting a little heroism into it. Especially when the story is about living through impossible hardship.

Memory is not an exact science. It does not work the same way for all people, or even from one day to the next. Some days you remember more, other days, less. For some people, events they read about in a book or saw in a movie will find their way into their dreams, and eventually their memories. I stand by during interviews to help people iron out these discrepancies.

Some people will naturally self-aggrandise. Occasionally, people will repeat stories that are amazing and heroic, and also completely impossible. It is natural to want to tell one's own story in a positive light.

When I'm helping record a testimonial and I hear something I know to be inaccurate, I will interrupt. I ask them: 'Are you *sure* it happened the way you are remembering it?'

This gives the witness a chance to think more slowly,

and to clarify. Even then, certain people, if they are that kind of character, will insist on making the story more exciting or intrepid than it was.

One survivor of the Vilna Ghetto, for instance, had a wonderful story about confronting a Nazi in the Ghetto with a hand grenade.

Now, I was in the Vilna Ghetto, and I never saw a hand grenade. It would have been impossible to find that kind of weaponry. So I asked, firmly but gently, 'Are you sure it was a hand grenade? I never saw a hand grenade in the Vilna Ghetto.'

And the man smiled and nodded, and said, 'Now that I think about it, perhaps it wasn't a hand grenade. Perhaps it was a rock.'

Then there are those who only survived by doing things that cause them shame, or that would distress their families too greatly to be made public. Now and again, a survivor gives a testimonial that they want sealed away until long after the end of their life.

The sad truth is, to have the best chance of survival, one had to be indispensable to the Nazis. We Jews all had to work for the Nazis, and if you didn't have some specific technical skill that would help keep their war machine operating, they did not believe you had the right to life.

Searching for the truth is very important in the work we do. Small misconceptions can easily become attached to memory and slowly unpick the seams of historical record. There are as many perspectives of the Holocaust as there are survivors. It's easy for someone unfamiliar with history to hear the story of one survivor and begin to think they are an expert, that the experience of that one individual can be extrapolated as universal history.

This is something we work to combat. We want to give no fuel to those who would deny us our legacy.

V

As time went on, it became more and more important that we bear witness. By the turn of the century there were already Holocaust deniers popping up, trying to convince the world that the Shoah never happened, or that it was not as horrific as we claim. Conspiracy theories were being circulated, claiming that the crimes of the Nazis and their allies were greatly exaggerated, or completely fabricated. Needless to say, this was very hurtful.

One Sunday morning I was at the Holocaust Centre when I heard someone hammering on the door. I was alone, quietly working on a video. When I answered the door, a man swept in and introduced himself in a rush. His name was Frederick, a Holocaust denier, and he had come to tell me 'the truth about history'.

For two hours he tried to convince me that the Holocaust never happened. He had a whole set of facts about a Jewish secret society that had perpetrated an elaborate hoax, faking the death of six million Jews in order to cheat the German government of reparations and to found the state of Israel. The man talked and talked without a break for the entire two hours—he didn't let me say one word. When he finished, the man left, sure he had persuaded me that it was all just an elaborate hoax.

What can you do in the face of that kind of thing? Not a great deal. At some point, for some reason, he had become converted to this conspiracy theory, and now his whole world view had been shaped to support it. There is no logic to the way humans act sometimes.

Even very educated and intelligent people can be uneducated in this matter. I knew of a German academic, Professor Dr Manfred Brewster, a lecturer of Criminology at Monash University. He had a sabbatical coming up, and decided that before returning to Germany, he would take time for a little travel around Australia.

One evening in Perth he visited a restaurant and found that almost all the meals on the menu were German. He started talking to the owner, a German refugee who had escaped to Australia before the war. After dinner, they ended up going back to his house. There, the restaurateur's mother-in-law started telling Dr Brewster about her experience in the German concentration camps. It was the first time he'd ever heard a first-hand account of the Holocaust.

This man was a respected professor who'd grown up in West Germany after the war, with no real idea of what his parents' generation had done. His eyes were opened.

When he returned to Melbourne, he came to visit the Holocaust Centre. It was a Sunday, and again I was the only one there. He stayed for a very long time, and I shared countless testimonials with him. After that, he began to do his part to record history and keep it alive for the next generation.

When he returned to his professorship in Germany, he began to research his own stories. He wrote a book chronicling Jewish lives lost in the Holocaust, and taught his students about the atrocities. Over the years we became very close friends. Every six months he would come to Melbourne to meet with me at the JHC, then we would dine together and discuss the legacy of the Holocaust at great length. On one visit, he asked me a question his students often had for him:

'Why does everyone describe the Holocaust differently? We hear so many people who were supposedly at Auschwitz at the same time and their stories don't quite match. How are we supposed to believe the facts of what happened if the stories aren't straight?'

I explained to him that the variety of survivors' experiences is proof that it happened. Memory is fallible. The years pass, and the trauma of what we experienced is something many of us would rather not carry with us. 'If everyone who saw me in this room remembered the Holocaust the exact same way, I would be suspicious,' I said. 'People only remember history the same way if they learned about it second-hand, instead of having lived it.'

It is impossible to understate the hurt that was done to us, nor how painful it is to carry that in silence for decades. The accumulated pain of not talking about the trauma for a lifetime marks a person.

When taking testimonials, often the whole story would explode out of someone, like a volcano erupting. Some people left the studio absolutely shattered by revisiting their memories and sharing their stories. But then, after a day or two, they began to slowly feel better. The pain of the release would be acute, but it would be temporary, and in many cases, afterwards, people started to heal.

People have the need to talk about their trauma. Sometimes when I picked someone up to take them to the studio they would begin talking and be unable to stop. On occasion, I've had to politely ask them to refrain until they are in front of the camera.

In 2008, Helen Leperere, one of my volunteers at the Holocaust Centre, along with my elder daughter, Michelle, nominated me for an Order of Australia. It was a lovely thought, which turned out to be quite a complicated process. The nomination required confirmation that the work of our Testimonies Project was held in esteem beyond our little corner of Melbourne. The Royal Panel ended up contacting organisations we worked with in the United States and Israel before deciding that I deserved the honour. In the end, some poor worker in the Australian Government had to go to the Israeli embassy to get a second opinion.

I was invited to a ceremony in the garden and grounds at Victoria's Government House, where I was given an Order of Australia Medal for community service.

You don't do this kind of work for recognition and awards from the government, but it doesn't hurt, either. It is very nice to know that the wider community appreciates the same values you work so hard to advance.

And I must admit, the OAM helped with the work. The prestige attached to it helped convince people to open doors and do us favours.

Another great personal honour was bestowed upon me in March 2011, when the JHC dedicated and named our collection the Phillip Maisel Testimonies Project. This moved me deeply. The work we do continues to give meaning to my life. That it also gives meaning to others is a wonderful thing.

And a treasured and unexpected honour was given to me in December 2019, when the JHC appointed me to the position of Life Governor—in appreciation of over thirty years of dedication to the centre.

VI

My team at the JHC are not the first to record the testimonials of survivors. First-hand accounts were taken by psychologists and journalists immediately after the Holocaust. The difference between the decades is startling. Reading early testimonies, the hatred is palpable—they were full of resentment towards the Germans and indicated a thirst for revenge. How could they do it? Why did they do it? It was baffling that such a technologically and culturally sophisticated society could be so barbaric. Years later, after decades of reflection and debate, there are no easy answers. But still, we search for reason. If one reads the interviews of survivors collected right after the war, many of them wanted revenge, for those responsible for the deaths of so many to be executed in turn. In time, people have mellowed, and the focus has turned to the quest for understanding, and to ensuring it never happens again.

In 1994, American filmmaker Steven Spielberg established the Shoah Foundation in America, a museum dedicated to the collection of first-person testimonials from survivors of the Holocaust.

Shortly after the foundation was established, a representative of the Shoah Foundation contacted me, proposing a collaboration between the Shoah Foundation and the JHC Testimonies Project. We met in Paris at a seminar on the Holocaust to discuss the possibility. However, while their research methodology was extremely good, I felt it was too different from our own philosophy to really work together well.

The greatest strength of the Testimonies Project at JHC comes from our sense of community, and building a relationship between interviewer and witness. The act of taking a person's testimonial is a great responsibility. The interviewer owes it to the survivor to be careful with their memories, and their trauma. When a testimony is given in a draughty shed with the rain drumming on the roof, it will be of a different quality to that given to a Hollywood film producer.

It is natural for people to embellish their stories, particularly if they are talking to a representative of the man who made *Schindler's List*. Talking to a member of your own community, in a quiet room, provides the kind of intimacy that allows someone to expose their flaws.

So, on that occasion I turned down the opportunity to collaborate with the Shoah Foundation.

In November 2019, the head of the Shoah Foundation, Dr Stephen Smith, was invited to Melbourne to speak on the commemoration of *Kristallnacht*—the famous 'Night of the Broken Glass'—the night of anti-Semitic attacks that was a prelude to the Holocaust. He was a very fine public speaker, and received a standing ovation.

I was very impressed by him, and after some discussion with my colleagues at the JHC, we decided to share our testimonials with the Shoah Foundation, and sent copies of our archives to America.

The Shoah Foundation was extremely well resourced, and used cutting-edge technology. They had a specially designed system that electronically supervised every testimony. The moment the recording starts to deteriorate, an electronic alert is sent to an archivist, who then take steps to correct it. This means their archives will remain in perfect condition for many, many years—and, I pray, for eternity. After all, ultimately, we have the same goal—to never forget.

VII

By the end of 1998, the JHC had expanded into a new, larger building, and over 180,000 Victorian schoolchildren had passed through its doors. The question of how young people would remember the Holocaust seemed increasingly urgent with the passing years. In time, would it become consigned to the history books, the scale of the atrocities fading as it passed from living memory?

The connection between visitors and survivor guides is invaluable. A face-to-face encounter with a Holocaust survivor is both disturbing and reassuring for young people, because the horrific truth of history is insulated by the storyteller's humanity.

I think often of my late friend Kitia Altman. She was from Bedzin, in Silesia, where the population was about 80 per cent Jewish. Caught up in the Holocaust, she worked in a local factory producing uniforms for the Wehrmacht. Alfred Rossner, the manager of the factory Kitia worked in, fell in love with her and saved her and her family from deportation many times. Eventually, Rossner was arrested by the Gestapo and sentenced to hanging, and Kitia was sent to a concentration camp.

She survived and settled in Melbourne, where she spent her retirement as a survivor guide at the JHC. Among the guides, she was legendary—a strong personality who could take a group of rowdy schoolchildren through the museum and have them treating her with absolute reverence by the end of the tour. When it came to the reality of her experience, she didn't mince words, which the students appreciated.

One child asked her: 'Did the Nazis ever rape you?'

'They didn't have to rape me,' she laughed. 'I would have gladly slept with any of them if they had a piece of bread.'

Kitia was fearless. When the English Holocaust denier David Irving visited Australia she challenged him to a debate on live television. She made short work of him. In the middle of a monologue about how his research had determined that Auschwitz was not a place of extermination she cut him off.

'Have you been there?'

'No.'

'I was. I can tell you all about it.'

On another occasion, the JHC was hosting an official discussion, debating the question, 'Where was God during the Holocaust?' Various prominent people from our community, religious and atheistic Jews presented their arguments.

All through the discussion Kitia sat quietly, but then she stood and called out: 'What does God have to do with it? You can't blame God for the Holocaust. It was people that did it all to us. Human beings just like you and me.'

She had a very forthright manner, and turned the whole conversation around. Kitia knew who was responsible for the Holocaust. She had looked them in the eye. For her, the question of God was irrelevant.

Of those who were religious before the Holocaust, some survivors lost their faith entirely. Others became even more devout as the years passed and they searched for meaning in what had happened to them.

Some very religious people blamed themselves, believing that the Holocaust was an Old Testament-style punishment from God for not being pious enough. I am not very religious myself, but I try to be open-minded. It is not always easy.

One day at the Holocaust museum, an Orthodox Jewish fellow, very religious, came to see me. He believed that the Holocaust was God's punishment for women dressing immodestly. He showed me a brochure for a local girls' school that featured the students wearing hockey uniforms, with their shoulders bared. He wanted me to agree that it was this kind of immodesty that brought the Shoah down on us.

I told him I respectfully disagreed with his beliefs and asked him to leave. He waited outside for two hours, until I took my lunch break, then followed me, trying to convince me. How could I argue with the fellow?

In some ways his views were as intractable as the

Holocaust denier who'd also ambushed me at the centre. His entire existence was framed around his faith, and he would always find ways to reinforce those beliefs.

We are human beings, and however we became the sentient creatures we are today, be it divine will or evolution, we are built with the need to believe in something supernatural, some power greater than ourselves.

VIII

There is a saying in medicine, an oath you take: 'First, do no harm.' This rule of thumb is the basis for all modern medicine—do no harm, even in the pursuit of help.

Remember that medical doctors were among the worst perpetrators of atrocities in the Holocaust. Take Auschwitz's Angel of Death, Dr Josef Mengele, who used the concentration camp as his own private laboratory to conduct cruel and bizarre experiments on children. He was obsessed with twins and developing a scientific method to impregnate women with more than one child at a time, in order to produce more Aryan children for Germany.

My friend and colleague from the JHC, Eva Slonim, was one of the children Mengele experimented on. She was twelve when she arrived at Auschwitz, along with her fifteen-year-old sister, but they looked so alike Mengele took them for twins, and selected them for painful, inhumane experiments.

When the prisoners of Auschwitz were sent on their death march, Eva was so weakened that she was abandoned, locked in a building that the Nazis put a torch to before fleeing. She should have burned to death, but a storm broke out, and a snowfall extinguished the fire. It is Eva's belief that the snowflakes that saved her were 'the *neshomot* (the souls of the victims) descending from heaven to save us.' Eva survived, and went on to migrate to Australia and establish a large family. Today, she has fifteen grandchildren, which she says are her revenge against the Nazis.

She organised for a special prayer room to be dedicated within our centre in which to honour and pay respect to those lost in the Holocaust. Her personal dedication was to the memory of her friend Moisze, a boy she befriended in Mengele's laboratories, who perished. When school groups come through, the guide will ask a volunteer to go into the prayer room and light a candle for Moisze and, in this small way, pay respect and keep his memory alive.

When Eva tells her story, I think of Moisze and the children who did not survive, and wonder if Dr Mengele really believed he was doing no harm, if he thought that he was making the world a better place through his cruelty.

IX

As I continued taking testimonials of survivors, my colleagues gave me a nickname—'The Keeper of Miracles'. It is an appropriate name, I think. I have been witness to countless stories that are nothing short of miraculous.

From time to time people ask me which testimonial has made the greatest impression on me. It is an impossible question. Each testimonial is important, and all of them for unique reasons. There is one that is never far from my mind, however.

It is an extraordinary story, of a woman who was a newborn baby when the deadliest days of the Holocaust began. Her Jewish parents knew they would not survive, so before the Nazis came for them, they gave their daughter to a Polish couple to raise her safely as their own.

They were a Catholic couple, and childless, although they very badly wanted a baby, and had prayed and prayed to be blessed with one. The husband fell in love with the adopted baby straight away, but the wife did not. The baby would not stop crying, she could not sleep, and the woman grew to resent her child more and more with each passing day.

One night, in the middle of the Polish winter, she took the baby outside and put her in the snow. The baby would freeze to death, and the woman could explain to her husband that it had been an accident—that the child had died in her sleep.

In the morning, she went outside to collect the body and found something shocking. The baby wasn't dead—far from it. She was smiling and kicking her little legs like she'd just woken up from a nap.

The Polish woman was sure this was a miracle, that God was teaching her a lesson. She was extremely religious, so, believing she was following the will of the Lord, she learned to accept the child, and raised her as a Polish Catholic.

The war ended and the child grew older, knowing nothing about her past. Then one day, by sheer coincidence, she happened to be out in the village with her adopted family when they heard a man introduce himself by the girl's original Jewish family name. The man was her uncle. He had survived the Holocaust and found a clue to her survival in Israel, so came back to the town seeking any trace of his dead family. And so, a second miracle occurred—she was reunited with her biological family, and with her Jewish heritage.

Two miracles, two impossible occurrences, each of them leading the girl not only to survive, but back to her family and her culture. It is not hard to imagine that there was some kind of higher power looking out for her.

It occurs to me that I have experienced many miracles in my life. The Lithuanian soldier who pretended he could not see us in the dark so that we could sneak into the Ghetto. The foreman in the garage who taught me how to repair vehicles, a skill that would save my life in Estonia. The day I lay down to die in the snow in my typhoid delirium, and somehow survived and then was nursed back to health. The time on the death march, when my friends risked their lives by stepping forward in the line to stop the SS murdering me. The fact that my brother and sister survived, and somehow, in a broken and chaotic post-war world, we found each other again. And the greatest of all—my family. To have the chance to marry and see my children grow up safe and happy.

Once you begin to look for the miracles in your life, you cannot stop finding them.

What ties these miracles together? I have thought long and hard about it, and I have an answer. Humanity. It is simple empathy. Each time my life was saved, it was because someone went out of their way to help me in my hour of need. What one person might interpret as incredible luck, and another might view as divine intervention, I see as humanity in its purest form.

Every 'miracle' I have experienced boils down to one thing—a human being, making a decision to reject hatred and fear, reaching out to help another, to save a life. I owe my life to these miracles. So does every survivor I have had the privilege of sitting with and listening to. It is not that I survived the Holocaust that is important, it is *how* I survived the Holocaust. None of us did it alone. The legacy of the Holocaust is one of fear, hatred and brutality, but it is also one of hope. This is one thing I know for certain. Hope is the only miracle we can be sure of in this world.

X

My life has been long. It is nearly a century since I came into this world, but I have few regrets. And most importantly to me, I have no regrets about my behaviour during the Holocaust.

I followed all the human principles, and I never consciously did anything to harm another human being. I was loyal to my friends; I risked my life to save them when I could. No matter how badly I was treated by the Germans, I never lost sight of the fact that they were people too, and that they were the ones who had given up their decency because of fear and greed. This gives me great solace.

What happened to me was terrible, but through it all, I managed to maintain my humanity. To be honest, it is this thought that kept me alive for many years—that as bad as things were, I was still a good man.

I truly believe that the human race will not survive unless we embrace our humanity. This means understanding that we are only a small part of an infinitely complex world, and that it is our duty to safeguard our small corner of it, and leave the world a better place than it was when we came in. This, I think, is something we can all do—but it is still miraculous.

I know that the next time I go to our little studio in the JHC and sit with a survivor of the Holocaust and begin to take their testimonial, I will find a miracle. I know that when I look through the lens of my camera I will begin to see the world through another survivor's eyes. Most importantly, the fact that we are both alive to share that moment—this, too, is a miracle. The fact that any of us survived. That fact that we can tell our story.

All the little miracles, the millions upon millions of them that accumulated in the survival of my people, and our culture. The memory of the millions of lives lost, the cities, towns and families destroyed. This is my responsibility and my privilege: to be custodian of their memories, to be able to pass their stories on to the next generation—for me, this will be the greatest miracle of all.

Epilogue

WHAT IS THE LESSON TO BE LEARNED FROM THE Holocaust? The question is impossible, there is no one answer. But our suffering does not have to be in vain. The world must learn not to succumb to fear and hatred, not to allow cynical propagandists to commit atrocities in the name of belief. This bias is built into all of humanity. This is what we must fight—we must endeavour to educate people, to give them the tools they need to recognise the truth of things. To recognise the lies that are created to take advantage of people's biases, because this is when good people can be driven to do terrible things.

Is this possible? I don't know. I once thought I could defeat the Nazis with a rifle. With the passing years, I have learned that there is only one way to defeat hatred, prejudice and ignorance. The question is, will people forget and do again what they did before? This seems to me the burning question of the past, and of the future. Our history is shared by all humanity—the lessons we must learn are the inheritance of the world.

When I first picked up a video camera at the JHC nearly thirty years ago, I felt—as I feel now—that the work is urgent. There are many reasons for this: to educate the young about the Holocaust, with the aim to prevent discrimination, racism and other genocides; to reignite the lives of communities that existed before the Holocaust; and for survivors to leave a legacy for their children and family. We are motivated by the need to bear witness, to find a little solace in the depths of tragedy. Attempts to discredit the history, to deny that these events occurred, can only be met with facts, and with tales of personal experiences that no one can refute.

In total, we have collected over 1700 testimonials. Each teaches us something new about the Holocaust, the world before it, and the world after. What I have learned from collecting testimonies is that we all have prejudices. Nobody is completely objective in the way they under-stand the shared experience. Everybody has a different pair of eyes, and it is very hard to see the world through someone else's.

The closest we can come is to listen to another person's story, to try to see the world the way they do for a while.

So, for as long as I am able, I will take my camera to our studio, and sit in a dark room and listen to a witness of our history.

It is important to remember that when we talk about the Holocaust, it is not only the history of what happened to the Jews. There were millions of victims from other religions, ethnic groups and minorities. It is their history too, all of the victims, as well as the history of the perpetrators and the collaborators. Each of their stories becomes a part of mine.

I hope that now, my story will become part of yours. This is my greatest wish: to educate, to give people the tools they need to walk away from hatred. This is what my story is for; what all our stories are for. To record—for history and for all that we lost—our humanity.

Acknowledgements

T HIS BOOK WOULD NOT HAVE BEEN POSSIBLE without the efforts and unwavering support of so many people.

First and foremost, I must thank my daughters Yvonne Sherwin and Michelle Deutsch, both for being the great joy in my life, and for helping me with my English, a language I am still perfecting! Thank you as well to their wonderful life partners, Ron Sherwin and Leon Deutsch; to my grandson, Robert Deutsch, who has been of great help while writing; and to Jason Sherwin and Nathan Deutsch, who have made me proud beyond measure to be their grandfather. Of course, I owe everything to my late wife, Miriam Maisel, who I hope I have done proud in telling our story.

It has been the great privilege in recent decades to serve as the custodian of testimonials for the Jewish Holocaust

Centre. The friendships I have enjoyed with my dear colleagues there have been instrumental in driving me to work every day at our vital task. I am grateful to all, too many to thank in one book, but I must single out Jayne Josem and Anna Hirsh who have been invaluable in helping to recount my story.

Endless gratitude must go to the many dedicated interviewers who have worked selflessly alongside me to record the legacy of the survivors.

I must thank Barbara Jarosz for kind company and care while writing this book.

And of course, I must thank the team at Pan Macmillan Australia for their tireless support, and especially my publisher Alex Lloyd for (convincing me to write this book in the first place!) his drive and vision, along with Liam Pieper for his assistance in helping me write my story. Special thanks to publicist Allie Schotte and marketer Adrik Kemp for helping share *The Keeper of Miracles* with Australia.

Finally, above all, I must thank you, the reader, for taking the time to share in my story, and the memory of the Shoah. It is with your help, that the memory of all survivors will live on. You are now part of my story. Please act, as I have tried to, as witness to history, and share our story with the world.